The Big Purple Book

*25 multi-purpose outlines
for pre-school groups*

© Scripture Union 2003

First published 2003

ISBN 1 85999 719 8

Scripture Union, 207–209 Queensway, Bletchley, MK2 2EB, England.

Email: info@scriptureunion.org.uk

Website: www.scriptureunion.org.uk

Scripture Union Australia, Locked bag 2, Central Coast Business Centre, NSW 2252

Website: www.su.org.au

Scripture Union USA, PO Box 987, Valley Forge, PA 19482

www.scriptureunion.org

Performing Licence

If you wish to perform any of the material in this book, you are free to do so without charge, providing the performance is undertaken in an amateur context. The purchase of this book constitutes a licence granting the right to perform the pieces for no financial gain. Those wishing to engage in commercial or professional performances should make a separate approach in writing to Scripture Union.

Unless otherwise stated, Bible quotations are from the Contemporary English Version © American Bible Society, published by HarperCollins Publishers, with kind permission from the British and Foreign Bible Society.

British Library Cataloguing-in-Publication Data: a catalogue record for this book is available from the British Library.

Scripture Union is an international Christian charity working with churches in more than 130 countries providing resources to bring the good news about Jesus Christ to children, young people and families – and to encourage them to develop spiritually through the Bible and prayer.

As well as a network of volunteers, staff and associates who run holidays, church-based events and school Christian groups, Scripture Union produces a wide range of publications and supports those who use the resources through training programmes.

Music books

JP	*Junior Praise* (Marshall Pickering)
JU	*Jump Up If You're Wearing Red* (NS/CHP)
KS	*Kidsource* (Kevin Mayhew)
LACH	*Let's All Clap Hands!* (Scripture Union)
LSS	*Let's Sing and Shout!* (Scripture Union)

Series editor: Maggie Barfield

Project manager: Louise Titley

Copy editor: Amy Leon

Writers: Maggie Barfield, Ruth Dell, Lynn Huggins-Cooper, Kevin and Val Moore, Judith Merrell, Priscilla Trood, Judith Wigley

Additional material: Jo Bailey, Mandy Catto, Liz Lunn, Susie Matheson, Val Mullally, Pam Priestley; 'See you soon' home time activity reprinted from *Playleader* magazine and used with permission

Cover and internal design by Mark Carpenter Design Consultants

Cover photography: Steve Shipman

Illustrations: Anna Carpenter

Printed and bound by Interprint Limited, Malta

Acknowledgements

Thank you to Christine Orme and Christine Wood for permission to use copyright material from *Splash*, SU 1992.

Some activities are based on material previously published in *Sing, Say and Move, Jigsaw, Let's Join In, Let's Praise and Pray, Let's Sing and Shout!* and *Let's All Clap Hands!* © Scripture Union.

Thank you to Val Mullally for creative help with the wood, stone and metal sessions.

Thank you to Diana Turner and Jackie Cray for so much valuable support and constructive comment.

Contents

Welcome to Tiddlywinks...

Remember the game? Play it anywhere, anytime with almost any age. It can be a two-minute time filler or an afternoon of family fun captivating even the youngest child's attention. Flipping, flying coloured discs, furious scrambles after lost 'winks' and triumphant laughter as three-year-old Lucy beats Grandad again! It's so simple, such fun.

Welcome to *Tiddlywinks*... resource material for young children that's fun, flexible, and extremely user-friendly.

Fun because it's child and therefore 'play' centred. The material reflects the understanding that young children grow, develop and learn through play. *Tiddlywinks* provides young children with a wide range of enjoyable, stimulating play experiences as a basis for learning about themselves, the world in which they live and the God who made both them and that world. It's designed to be good fun!

Flexible because it is adaptable to almost any situation. The work of the Christian church is no longer restricted to Sundays as literally thousands of carers and their young children flock through the doors of our churches, halls, and community buildings between Monday and Friday. Thankfully church leaders are waking up to the fact that what happens midweek really matters, and these people are being increasingly valued as members of the extended church family. That in no way devalues the very important work that goes on during a Sunday, both within the framework of a service of worship or Sunday teaching group. BOTH Sunday and midweek work are important and of equal value, but material that's easily adaptable to a variety of different

contexts needs to be flexible. *Tiddlywinks* has been written and designed with that flexibility in mind. Whether you are responsible for a midweek carer and toddler group, pram service (more likely to be called something like Butterflies, Minnows or Little Angels!), or you are a leader in a playgroup or nursery class, overseeing a Sunday crèche, teaching an early years Sunday group class, or part of a community based play centre or shoppers' crèche – there is material in *Tiddlywinks* that will be adaptable to your situation. Some of you will be looking to fill a two-hour programme, others two minutes! *Tiddlywinks*' pick-and-mix style is here to meet the needs of a wide range of contexts.

User-friendly because it is accessible to leaders who are just starting out as well as those with more experience. Whether you're wondering how to tell a Bible story, wanting to learn age-appropriate rhymes and songs, looking for creative ideas for prayer or wondering how telling the story of Noah might fit in with your early learning goals, *Tiddlywinks* can help you.

Tiddlywinks places great importance upon relationships. It recognises the crucial role of parents, carers and leaders in the development of a young child in his or her early years and the need to support and encourage all who share in this important task. Friendship between adults and children creates community, identity and a sense of belonging. When that community becomes a safe place where trust and friendship grow, both adults and children thrive within it. There could be no better foundation in the life of a young child.

OK, but you still have questions

Each outline has an activity page which can be used either in the group or at home. Photocopy as many pages as you need. Some of the craft activities recommended on these pages will work better if you photocopy them directly onto thin card instead of onto paper. Encourage adults to talk about the leaflets with the children and to do the activities together.

If the sheet is taken home, you could photocopy your group news or notices onto the blank reverse.

Where do I start…? How do I use it…? Who can use it…? Where can it be used…? When is the best time…? Why introduce spiritual topics to young children at all…? Do I need special equipment…? What skills will I need…? Will it cost anything…? Who will come…?

Everyone who has worked with young children has asked these and many other questions at some stage! The writers of *Tiddlywinks* are firmly convinced that adults learn through experience too.

In fact, 'hands-on' is the very best way to learn! No academic or paper qualification can replace first-hand experience of simply being and engaging with young children as they play and learn. The best qualifications for working with young children are a desire to be with them and a willingness to learn.

The following pages are here to help you think through questions you may have, guide your planning and preparation and help you get the best for your children from *Tiddlywinks*. We start with the all-important question WHY? If you are convinced of the reasons for working with young children, developing body, mind and spirit, you will keep going even when it feels tough. Conviction produces commitment and determination, qualities worth cultivating in any children's leader. And *Tiddlywinks* is here to help. Enjoy it!

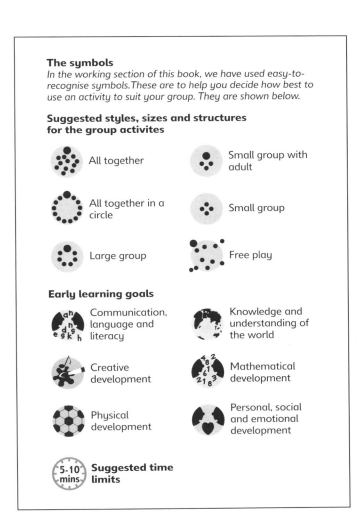

The symbols
In the working section of this book, we have used easy-to-recognise symbols. These are to help you decide how best to use an activity to suit your group. They are shown below.

Suggested styles, sizes and structures for the group activites

All together

Small group with adult

All together in a circle

Small group

Large group

Free play

Early learning goals

Communication, language and literacy

Knowledge and understanding of the world

Creative development

Mathematical development

Physical development

Personal, social and emotional development

Suggested time limits 5–10 mins

Why?

Why work with babies, toddlers and pre-schoolers? Why go to such lengths to provide appropriate play facilities, resources and materials for such young children? Let's be honest; they are noisy, messy, sometimes smelly, and thoroughly exhausting!

But, as the psalmist reminds us, they are also very special, a gift from God:

*You are the one who put me together
inside my mother's body,
and I praise you
because of the wonderful
        way you created me.*

(Psalm 139:13,14)

Few of us would deny the wonder of a new baby. The sense of miracle is often overwhelming and awe inspiring, and it isn't difficult to believe in a Creator God at such times. But the real truth behind the psalmist's words is that God's mark is upon each and every one of us right from the very beginning. From conception each one is a unique, individual human being, made in the image of God.

God's image within us is spiritual, and children (especially young children), are spiritual beings in their own right. As leaders, parents or carers of young children God gives us the awesome responsibility of sharing in his creation process. As the children in our care grow in body, mind and spirit, we become partners with God in that developmental process. Research tells us that the first five years of a child's life are the most crucial, laying down important foundations for the rest of life. If that is so, we know that we face quite a challenge. The stimulus we provide, the environment in which they grow, the quality of relationships and the values they experience will make an enormous difference to the children in our care.

Good relationships between young children and their carers are crucial for healthy growth and development. A child who experiences love, trust, security and forgiveness in their closest human relationships will quickly understand about the God who also loves, cherishes, protects and forgives them. When they become part of a community that lives out those values the impact is even greater. Their experience will make sense of all they will come to learn through the many Bible stories they hear; stories that reflect those same values and truths. When a group both practices and teaches these values it becomes a powerful place of spiritual learning for all who are part of that community. Young children and their parents and carers will thrive and grow in body, mind and spirit.

When fostered at an early age the relationship between a young child and God is transparently beautiful, often uncomplicated and spontaneous. Children are often more in touch with their spirituality than adults. They sense, they feel, they wonder but don't necessarily express those things in words. Their experience of God doesn't always need words. On several occasions in the Gospels Jesus used children as an illustration of those to whom the kingdom of God belonged, encouraging adults to 'become as a child' in order to enter that kingdom (Luke 18:15–17; Mark 10:13–16; Matthew 19:13–15).

Many adults' lives have been greatly influenced by the faith of a child. By sharing in their experiences, teaching them appropriately, guiding them gently, and enabling them to grow in body, mind and spirit they too have come to a greater understanding of God, his relationship with us and plan and purpose for our lives. We live in an age where two, almost three generations of adults have had little or no positive teaching about God or experience of the church. Many of these are the parents of the children in our pre-school groups. Some of us reading these introductory pages (including the writer!) will not have received a Sunday school education but others will have been nurtured in the Christian faith from the cradle. Many of the stories we share with our children will be new to us. The action rhymes and songs of praise may be the first 'hymns' we have ever sung. Many of the ideas for prayer will be our introduction to prayer. It's a whole new journey, one in which our children will undoubtedly lead us, but a journey which, in hindsight, we shall all travel together.

Why share spiritual truths with young children? Because we all want the very best for our children and in seeking to provide the best we are all privileged to learn from them in the process.

Where and when?

Where and when you use *Tiddlywinks* material will vary considerably, as will the extent of the use of the material provided. Each session incorporates different child-centred activities linked by a theme: Play time; Game time; Making time; Story time; Rhyme time; Song time; Pray time. You may be in a position to influence everything that happens in your group and therefore, make use of any number of these. Alternatively you may have responsibility for one part of your group's programme, eg the singing time, a craft activity, or story time. The joy of *Tiddlywinks* is that you can simply extract what you need for use at any one time.

Let's look at the variety of different contexts in which pre-school groups meet and the way in which they might use *Tiddlywinks* material:

Midweek 'pram' services
Tiddlywinks contains all that a leader might need for these short, midweek 'services' of worship for pre-school children. Time may prevent them from using all the material and lack of suitable facilities may restrict the type of Play time and Making time, especially if these groups meet inside the main body of their church (although there are a number of ingenious and creative ways of adapting what might at first seem insurmountable obstacles). But, provided they have an area in which they can move safely and sit comfortably together, Game, Story, Pray, Rhyme and Song time will be ideal for these occasions.

Midweek parent/carer and toddler groups
These important groups provide a much needed meeting point in the community particularly for first time parents and carers of young children. They are led by a wide range of people, including leaders formally appointed by the church, Christian mums who attend the group with their own children, and mums, or carers, who have little contact with the church but who use (often renting) church buildings as a meeting place.

Some will run along very similar lines to pram services seeking to provide a place where Christian values will be experienced and the faith taught. Others will simply be seeking to provide quality play and creative stimulation for the children present. *Tiddlywinks* material can meet both of these needs with leaders carefully selecting what they feel is appropriate for their situation. Whilst each section is thematically linked it can also stand on its own. Linking a five-minute craft activity with a ten-minute singing time may be all that is required whilst others will incorporate a story and prayer time. It is totally flexible.

Sunday groups
Many Sunday crèches and early years teaching groups (usually for children aged two-and-a-half to five years) will be looking for a balanced teaching programme to follow over a set number of different weeks, covering the whole of the church's festivals and seasons. These children will generally come from Christian homes and families where the faith is lived as well as taught. *Tiddlywinks* will offer an extensive range of topics and themes ideally suited to this context, and of course the teaching and learning style is always child-centred and age appropriate.

Playgroups and nurseries
Most playgroups and nurseries for two-and-a-half to five-year-olds are officially registered with OFSTED and seek to follow the early years educational goals and guidelines. Leaders are trained and fully responsible for the children in their care. Whilst not written with the sole intention of meeting the educational requirements of these goals, much of the material will serve to enhance and supplement the curriculum required for these groups.

Informal settings, eg coffee mornings and drop-in centres
These informal and casual places of meeting provided by many churches regularly attract young children but rarely provide adequate facilities for them. Following five minutes of biscuit munching they are bored and restless. A simple craft activity, a couple of songs and rhymes, and a short story can make their brief visit a very valuable experience. It's a statement about how much we value these children as well as a valuable teaching opportunity. It also encourages them to return.

Special events
Many churches recognise that what happens on a Sunday morning is often inaccessible and inappropriate to young children and their families. But this does not always mean that there is not an interest in learning about and experiencing the Christian faith. Many groups are experimenting with occasional events geared entirely for young families at a time that is suitable for them. Some have found Saturday tea times a good meeting time, others Sunday afternoons. Festivals, ie Christmas, Easter, Harvest etc are excellent starting points for these and often draw large numbers of people, especially when food is part of the programme. The *Tiddlywinks* special feature (designed for big group events – see pages 90 and 91) and/or *Tiddlywinks* session material can be creatively used to provide a theme base with all the necessary ingredients for an enjoyable family-friendly programme.

How?

How?

When setting out to run a group for pre-school children and their carers there are practical things to consider which are essential, others that are recommended and others still that are a bonus. This page outlines all three. It also includes a recommended plan of action for any who might be starting from scratch.

ESSENTIAL

Health and safety

Imagine the building to be used for the group as your own home and apply the same levels of health and safety requirements. Check heaters, floor surfaces, furniture, plug sockets, secure entry and exit points, fire exits, toilet and baby changing facilities, kitchen hygiene and safety if serving refreshments. Be aware of the different allergies that could affect children and encourage leaders to attend a First Aid course. Aim for the highest possible standards of health and safety at all times.

Child Protection

In the UK, the 1989 Children's Act is designed to encourage good practice and safety in all work undertaken with children aged 0–18 years of age, including that in churches. Any church-sponsored group where children remain in the care of leaders for longer than two hours, and which meets more than six times a year, is required to register with the Social Services department of the local authority. Many of our playgroups and nurseries fall into this category, but parent/carer and toddler groups do not need to register, although many choose to notify local authorities of their existence. Where parents and carers remain with their children for the duration of the session they are held responsible for their own children. Each church denomination or network has drawn up its own guidelines for good practice with recommendations for group leaders working in this context. These can be obtained from national headquarters or through regional children's advisers and should be followed carefully in order to maintain the highest of standards possible.

If you are working outside the UK, please check up on the Child Protection legislation for your area.

Insurance cover

Insurance for pre-school groups should have appropriate and adequate cover. Existing church policies should always be checked. Specialist agencies such as the *Pre-School Learning Alliance* or *Playgroup Network* work with major insurance companies to provide tailor-made packages for pre-school groups.

RECOMMENDED

Storage facilities

You can never have enough storage! What might start as one plastic box full of toys and materials will quickly multiply. Borrow, beg, plead and cry for more boxes, shelves, cupboards, and storerooms that are easily accessible; make setting out and clearing away as easy as possible.

Keeping records

The fire service require a written record of all persons in a public building at any time which provides a very useful record of all who have attended. Additional information such as addresses, phone numbers, birth dates help to inform members in the event of unexpected group closure due to bad weather or sickness, and to acknowledge birthdays of children, all of which shows care and concern. Ensure, however, that confidentiality is maintained with all personal details kept on file. In accordance with the Data Protection Act, do not divulge any information to third parties.

A photocopiable registration form can be found on the inside front cover of *Tiddlywinks: The Big Red Book*.

Teamwork

This work requires storytellers, singers, craft specialists, people who will keep a register, take monies, make refreshments, set out and clear away, etc. Where teamwork is fostered it also becomes a training ground for future leaders: those making coffee may develop into wonderful storytellers, songwriters or craft workers. Try to create an atmosphere where people are free to learn and you will grow your own leaders naturally.

Budgeting

Much of this work incorporates both the spiritual nurture of children and outreach to carers and families. Many churches allocate a specific amount of budget money for this purpose but don't always recognise the context in which it is being done. Be sure to remind them and ask for ongoing financial support to fund the work. Training leaders, publicity, resource books, craft materials, play equipment, refreshments and various other miscellaneous items can be costly. Keep a record of expenditure and income, with proof of purchases at all times. Don't be worried about making a charge for the group, as many parents/carers are more than willing to contribute towards something that their children enjoy.

BONUS

Behind the scene helpers

There are many housebound people in our churches who love to be involved in children's work. Publicity, programmes and newsletters can be designed on computers; craft materials cut and prepared well in advance and prayer can be a vital and encouraging support to a tired and weary leader. A little advance planning can alleviate a lot of pressure when shared with willing home-based workers.

Outside funding

Occasionally groups have benefited from charitable grants. Different bodies vary considerably in the criteria set out for funding – many decline groups that promote religious activities whilst others seem much more open. Local libraries usually have details of local and national charities.

If starting your group from scratch you should always seek the permission and support of your church leadership body. Go equipped with a well thought through plan of action.

Playing with a purpose

Play is the basis for almost every part of the *Tiddlywinks* material because the writers know and understand that young children learn everything through playing. Their capacity to listen is limited to just one minute for each year of life and so the suggestions offered include very few 'listening only' activities. In recent years educationalists have confirmed that all ages of children and adults learn far more through what they do and experience than simply through what they hear.

Each part of the theme-based *Tiddlywinks* programme is designed to offer young children some kind of play with a purpose. As a child moves from one activity to another, joining in small and large group experiences, he or she is gathering understanding and experience of that topic or theme. Of course some won't make the connections, but others will.

What is most important is that each activity is accessible and meaningful and it is the leader's task to provide the basic ingredients and stimulus for creating the best possible, purposeful play experience. Let's consider the different play sections of the programme:

Play time

(unstructured play)
'Play time' describes a variety of unstructured play activities, many of which will connect with children's every day life and experiences. This is likely to take up the bulk of the session and greet children on arrival. It will help introduce them to the day's topic, eg animals for story of Noah, boats for story of Jesus and the storm, food for story of feeding 5,000, etc, and acquire the vocabulary (when stimulated by adults) for use in the songs and rhymes, and explore concepts, eg animal families, effects of water, sharing out food between friends and dolls. All these play experiences are valuable in their own right but also become important foundations in a programme designed to help young children learn about a specific Christian story or Bible truth.

Game time

(cooperative play)
Young children generally play alone but simple, non-competitive games will develop an awareness of others and a sense of belonging to a group. They will learn to share, take turns, watch (and imitate) others, express delight in both their own and others' achievements, and respond to each other. Physically active games also stimulate physical development especially coordination and balance. Games can strengthen relationships within a group and help create a community built on Christian values, as well as provide a greater understanding and experience of the story or theme being developed.

Story time

(engaging play)
When creatively led, a story time demands much more than just listening. Most Bible stories lend themselves to visual, sound and action aids, actively engaging as many of the children's senses as you possibly can. Participation will involve ears, voices, hands (and legs) but also the emotions. Young children will live through the characters they are introduced to, imagining, feeling, sensing, and exploring all aspects of the story you are telling. They may not be able to respond with words but they will be learning.

Making time

(creative play)
Creative play introduces young children to a whole new world. The learning here most definitely takes place in the process of making and not in the end product, even though it will be greatly cherished and a very important reminder of the day's theme or story. Size, shape, texture, colour and patterns are just some of the important discoveries that will be made through making. Children will explore a variety of materials and acquire new skills and techniques. Together parents, carers and children will grow in confidence and creativity; they will uncover the mark of a creative God within them, in whose image they have been made. Whatever the limitations on your space and facilities make 'Making time' possible, as it is one of the most valuable learning experiences of all.

Song time and Rhyme time

(musical play)
Music, rhythm, rhyme and movement are experiences of the womb so it's not surprising that even the youngest of babes will actively respond to this part of the programme. When part of a circle time the learning is far more than simply the words of songs and rhymes being used. Young children learn to listen, follow actions, take turns, recognise each other and be part of a group experience. Even those who appear not to be participating amaze parents by repeating everything they have learnt hours later when at home!

Adults too

Never underestimate all that adults are learning through the children's play programme. Some are actually learning how to play themselves; others are learning Bible stories and truths for the first time; and others will want to develop that learning through further adult-centred programmes. *Tiddlywinks* even provides suggestions for ways in which you might help them to do so.

Making the most of structure

Under-fives love routine and structure. They learn through rhythm and repetition. It makes them feel secure and safe and helps them to quickly identify people, situations and experiences. As these become positive experiences children will look for them, ask for them and sometimes be very difficult to handle when they don't get them!

Structure doesn't mean boring repetition or inflexibility. It is determined by the basic needs of the children in our care. Every child needs to eat (even if they don't want to!) and so the structure of our day includes several eating times, but, exactly when, where and what we eat is determined by the individual's needs and circumstances. In the same way, a group including young children and their carers needs to have a structure that has been fashioned and shaped to meet the needs and circumstances of its members.

Tiddlywinks material is shaped into a structure that incorporates several important components; 'welcome' time; 'circle' time and 'home' time. Each are created to produce familiarity and security for both carers and children.

Welcome time

Providing a welcome is all about creating a sense of belonging, being part of a community. The key to doing it lies in being ready. Try out the ideas on pages 92 and 93.

Ready for children

The room or area being used should act like a magnet to every child so that they are immediately drawn into a play activity of some kind. Pre-schoolers are not able to sit around waiting for everyone to arrive! They need to play. When setting out your room make safe provision for babies and early toddlers, keep large pieces of equipment and mobile toys away from activity tables and encourage adult participation by positioning chairs close to activity tables.

Ready for adults

Establishing eye contact and welcoming individuals by name are the two most important acts of welcome. A one-to-one personal approach helps adults feel they and their children belong to a caring community. It reflects the love and care that Christians know God has for each individual.

Ready for newcomers

Newcomers need special treatment. First experiences are lasting ones and once put off they rarely give you a second chance. A leader should be allocated specifically to the task of welcoming new adults and children. Often there are details that need to be taken and procedures to explain which take time. It can also be helpful to provide a little leaflet describing the group, its purpose and structure, giving useful contact numbers.

Tiddlywinks provides a number of suggestions for activities that help build a sense of welcome. Remember whatever you choose, it will necessitate you being ready – the most important welcome factor of them all!

Circle time

Circle time is all about communication, for which you will need to be prepared. It's about preparing any number of the story, rhyme, song and prayer activities suggested in the *Tiddlywinks* material to engage both children and adults within a simple circle. The 'circle' shape is important as it includes everyone and brings them into a position where they can see and join in with what is happening. Participation by everyone is crucial to the success of circle time and many groups choose to go into a separate area or room to avoid distractions of toys and equipment; others simply clear away before starting. This time is key to developing the sense of belonging and group ownership from which will grow shared responsibility and strong community ties.

When you are part of a community you share special occasions together. It may be a birthday (adult's or child's!), special anniversary (of the group or church) or celebration of a newborn baby. Circle time is the ideal time to focus on these special occasions. There may also be sad times for which the group as a whole need to find an expression of shock, grief or sorrow, eg bereavement of a child, a national tragedy, a local concern. The simple lighting of a candle, a song or prayer may be sensitively incorporated into this special time together.

Home time

So far, creating our structure has involved being ready and being prepared. Ensuring a positive home time means we have to be organised. Too often under-fives groups simply disintegrate with no positive means of finishing or saying goodbye. People drift away as leaders scurry around tidying up. A positive ending gives a feeling of satisfaction and completion and develops a sense of anticipation for the next meeting.

Many group sessions end with a circle time building in a final song or rhyme that indicates 'this is the end'. *Tiddlywinks* offers a number of different ways in which you can mark the end in this way. Look at the ideas on pages 94 and 95 and try to choose one that best suits your group, and let it become part of your routine.

Quick tips to get you started...

Many experienced children's leaders find working with groups of young children daunting, especially when parents and carers are present. The skills and confidence required are quite different to those needed to work with older children. If you are new to this age range, or it has been some years since you've had contact with them, spend some time simply being with them and familiarising yourself with their behaviour and play patterns. You will be amazed at how quickly you acquire the knowledge and experience necessary for leading various parts of the *Tiddlywinks* programme. Here are a few tips to get you started:

● Using the Bible with young children

Do explain that the Bible is God's very special storybook

Do show the children a child-friendly Bible each time you tell a Bible story so that they become familiar with it

Do make it accessible to them and encourage them to borrow a copy to take home

Don't read straight from the Bible, always 'tell' a story

Do communicate an enthusiasm and excitement for the stories you tell, remembering that you share God's story

Do be prepared for the many questions that some children will ask!

● Storytelling

Do make it short (remember one minute of attention for each year of a child's life)

Do sit where you can see and be seen

Do make it visual, eg large pictures, household objects, puppets, Duplo, or toys

Do involve the children in actions, sounds, and repetitive phrases

Do give them time and space to respond to the stories with their comments and questions

Don't be worried about repeating the story, especially if they have enjoyed it!

● Leading songs and rhymes

Don't worry about not being able to play an instrument

Do sit at the children's level when leading

Don't teach more than one new song at any one time

Don't pitch songs and rhymes too high or use complex tunes

Do use children's instruments but,

Don't forget to put them away afterwards

Do encourage parents and carers to join in

Do use familiar tunes and write your own words

● Behaviour

Do make sure that parents and carers know they are responsible for their children

Do offer support to a parent/carer whose child is going through a difficult stage

Don't discuss the behaviour of their child in front of others

Do remember there is nearly always a reason for bad behaviour, eg boredom, neglect, inappropriate play, tiredness, hunger etc

Do develop positive strategies for dealing with common behaviour patterns in young children, eg biting, pushing, unwillingness to share, tantrums, dirty nappies!

Do encourage parents and carers to deal with difficult behaviour and

Don't intervene unless a child is in danger

● Craft

Do protect tables, floors and children if using messy materials

Do supervise at all times

Do let the children do the activity! (Provide additional materials if adults want a go.)

Don't worry too much about the end product

Do have hand-washing facilities ready

Don't allow the activity to go on too long

Do create drying space for activities needing to dry

Do be sure to put the child's name on the activity at the start

Do allow children to take them home – make more if you need a display

Do make the most of creating displays – it is a presence of the group in their absence

● Prayer

Do make prayers short, simple and spontaneous

Do try using a candle, bell or simple prayer song to introduce a prayer time

Do encourage different kinds of prayer, eg 'thank you', 'sorry' and 'please' prayers

Don't always insist on hands together, eyes closed

Do encourage action, rhyme and song prayers

Don't miss the opportunity to send written prayers into the home through craft activities

Do consider writing your own special prayer for the group that the children can learn and grow familiar with

● Involving parents and carers

Do spend time fostering good friendships with parents and carers

Do make clear to them that they are responsible for their children

Do encourage maximum participation at all times

Don't expect a parent/carer with more than one child to carry responsibility for activities

Do look out for hidden talents and leadership skills

Don't reject genuine offers of help and support

Do affirm, support and encourage parents and carers at all times.

Working with young children is hard work but we gain far more than we ever give. Be warned – shopping in your local supermarket will never be the same again. You will be gurgled at, sung to, waved at and clearly shouted at from one end of the freezers to the other. Entering the world of young children in your community will provide you with a whole new family! And together you will become part of God's family.

Additional resources
to help and support you in your work with young children and their parents/carers.

Recommended children's Bibles and storybooks

The Beginner's Bible (Zondervan)

The Lion First Bible (Lion Publishing)

Lift the Flap Bible (Candle Books)

Me Too! Books, Marilyn Lashbrook (Candle Books) 16 different titles with interactive stories from both the New and Old Testament

Tiddlywinks: My Little Red Book – First Steps in Bible Reading, Ro Willoughby; *My Little Blue Book*, Penny Boshoff; *My Little Yellow Book*, Leena Lane and Penny Boshoff; *My Little Green Book*, Christine Wright, *My Little Purple Book*, Jo Bailey (Scripture Union)

Action Rhyme series, Stephanie Jeffs (Scripture Union) 4 titles:
Come into the Ark with Noah; March Round the Walls with Joshua; Follow the Star with the Wise Men; Share out the Food with Jesus

Bible Concertina books, Nicola Edwards and Kate Davies (Scripture Union)
The Creation; Noah's Ark; The Christmas Baby

The Bible Pebbles series, Tim and Jenny Wood (Scripture Union) *Daniel in the Lion's Den; Jonah and the Big Fish; Moses in the Basket; Noah's Ark; The First Christmas; The First Easter; Jesus the Healer; Jesus the Teacher*

The Little Fish series, Gordon Stowell (Scripture Union). Lots of titles about Jesus, other Bible people, and you and me.

Jigsaw Bible Activity Books 2, 3 and 4 (Scripture Union)

Things Jesus Did, Stories Jesus Told, People Jesus Met, Baby Jesus, Stephanie Jeffs (Bible Reading Fellowship)

Prayer books

Pray and Play: 101 Creative Prayer Ideas for Use with Under-fives, Kathy L Cannon (Scripture Union)

The Pick a Prayer Series, Tim and Jenny Wood, illustrated by Suzy-Jane Tanner (Scripture Union), 4 spiral-bound board titles:
Pick-a-prayer: For Bedtime; Pick-a-prayer: For Every Day; Pick-a-prayer: For Special Days; Pick-a-prayer: To Say Thank You

My Little Prayer Box, (Scripture Union)

Hello God, it's Me, Stephanie King and Helen Mahood (Scripture Union)

The Lion Book of First Prayers, Sue Box (Lion Publishing)

What Shall We Pray About? Andy Robb (Candle)

Prayers with the Bears, (John Hunt Publishing) 4 titles

101 Ideas for Creative Prayer, New Ideas for Creative Prayer, Judith Merrell (Scripture Union)

Song/rhyme books

Let's Sing and Shout! ed. Maggie Barfield (Scripture Union)

Let's All Clap Hands! ed. Maggie Barfield (Scripture Union)

Jump Up If You're Wearing Red (NS/CHP)

Feeling Good!, Peter Churchill (NS/CHP)

Bobby Shaftoe, Clap your Hands, Sue Nicholls, (A&C Black) includes 37 familiar and traditional tunes with simple guitar chords.

Kidsource Books 1 and 2 (Kevin Mayhew). A general selection for children, including many suitable for under-fives.

Other resources

God and Me series, exploring emotions and Christian beliefs (Scripture Union):
Really, Really Scared; Really, Really Excited; I Love You; I Miss You, Leena Lane
What's Heaven Like?; What's God Like?; What's in the Bible?; Can Jesus Hear Me? Stephanie King

Resources to support parents and carers

Lion Pocketbook Series, various authors (Lion Publishing). Over 15 different titles on both faith-searching issues, eg *Why Believe?; Why Pray?*, and pastoral issues, eg *Why Marry?; When a child dies*. These are inexpensive pocketbooks ideal for use with parents and carers.

First Steps, video for parents inquiring about infant baptism, (CPAS)

Welcome to Baptism, Journey of a Lifetime Video, Grayswood Studio

Time out for Parents, Positive Parenting Publications, First Floor, 2A South Street, Gosport PO12 1ES. A comprehensive teaching pack, covering most aspects of parenting from infancy to teenage years

Just a Minute: Biblical Reflections for Busy Mums, Christine Orme (Scripture Union)

Family Caring Trust
Director: Michael Quinn, 44 Rathfriland Rd, Newry, Co. Down, N Ireland BT34 1LD
The Family Caring Trust produce an extensive range of parenting courses focusing on different age ranges of children. These have been widely used and appreciated in pre-school community groups.

CARE for the Family PO Box 448 Cardiff CF15 7YY
CARE produce a wide range of resources to support parents including a video based course called Parent Talk, books, training and special parent and child weekends.

Courses for parents/carers who wish to explore questions and issues of faith:

Emmaus, National Society

Alpha, Holy Trinity Brompton

Additional leaders' resource material

SALT 3 to 4+ for leaders and *Sparklers* activity material for children (Scripture Union)

Tiddlywinks: The Big Red, Blue, Yellow and Green Books/My Little Red, Blue, Yellow and Green Books (Scripture Union)

Glitter and Glue: 101 Creative Craft Ideas for Use with Under-fives, Annette Oliver (Scripture Union)

Praise Play and Paint, Jan Godfrey (NS/CHP)

Under Fives Alive and *Under Fives – Alive and Kicking*, Farley, Goddard, Jarvis, (NS/CHP)

Bible Fun for the Very Young, Vicki Howe (Bible Reading Fellowship)

Bible Stuff, Janet Gaukroger (CPAS) 5 titles in the series.

The following 2 titles are packed with ideas for encouraging parents and children to celebrate the Christian year at home:
Feast of Faith, Kevin and Stephanie Parkes (NS/CHP)
The 'E' Book, Gill Ambrose (NS/CHP)

Background reading

Working with Under 6s, Val Mullally (Scripture Union)

Children Finding Faith, Francis Bridger (Scripture Union/CPAS)

Bringing Children to Faith, Penny Frank (Scripture Union/CPAS)

Children and the Gospel, Ron Buckland (Scripture Union)

The Adventure Begins, Terry Clutterham (Scripture Union/CPAS)

Seen and Heard, Jackie Cray (Monarch)

Sharing Jesus with Under Fives, Janet Gaukroger (Crossway Books)

Networks and organisations supporting work with young children

Pre-school Learning Alliance
61-63 Kings Cross Rd, London WC1X 9LL

Playgroup Network, PO Box 23, Whitley Bay, Tyne and Wear, NE26 3DB

Scripture Union
207-209 Queensway, Bletchley, Milton Keynes, MK2 2EB. www.scriptureunion.org.uk
For readers in other countries, please contact your national Scripture Union office for details.

The Mothers' Union
24 Tufton St, London SW1P 3RB

Church Pastoral Aid Society
Jackie Cray, Adviser for Families and Under-fives, Athena Drive, Tachbrook Park, Warwick CV34 6NG

How to plan your group programme using Tiddlywinks

Tiddlywinks Big Books provide resources, ideas and activities for use in any pre-school setting. Whether you are running a carer-and-toddler group; a playgroup or pre-school; a nursery or nursery school; a child-minding network; a crèche or toddler club; a conventional Sunday morning group at church; a drop-in centre; a coffee morning or a pram service or any other group where under-fives gather – *Tiddlywinks* has suggestions to help you.

Here, some pre-school practitioners choose their own options for their own different types of group, using the topic 'Jesus stops a storm' on pages 38, 39 and 42.

Jo leads a toddler group which meets on Friday mornings; once a month at the end of the session, everyone goes into the church for a 15–20 minute pram service. About 20 children are involved and their ages range from six months to three years. Jo says, 'Our pram service builds on what we've been doing in the toddler play session. Other weeks we don't have a story but we would still have songs and rhymes to remind the children of what we've been doing.'

Jo's choice

Most of our session is free play, supervised by the adults who bring the children so we'd use these ideas. We'd include the game suggestion as part of free play too. The Making time might need simplifying as the children are very young, but I'd like to use it. The story would be used in the pram service part of the session, when we usually tell a story. We find songs to well-known tunes work very well, but would probably do a simpler prayer than the one given. I'd probably use the rhyme, but maybe not if we'd told the story. We wouldn't have time for the extra ideas, but we may use them another week. I'd certainly take on board what's said in Adults too though I'm not sure how I would use it. Most of our children are too young for the activity page, although I may have a few copies for any older ones who come.

Mary is a teacher of a reception class of 4- and 5-year-olds at a church school. She also leads the 'Sparklers' group for pre-school children at her church.

Mary's choices

For reception class

We have a strong emphasis on learning through play so I like the variation in the play ideas and the way this is shown as a 'free choice' activity. The craft activity looks great, but would need too much adult supervision to be suitable for our classroom. There is great dramatic storytelling involving all the children in role play. The rhyme and song reinforce this; I like the way the song fits a familiar tune. We wouldn't use the prayer idea in this setting. The filler activities in Extra time are all good. Plus the activity page is a good literacy activity. I'll certainly ask the school to buy a copy of this book!

For 'Sparklers'

Free play is impractical in our church hall and our time is very limited. I would use the game and have it ready to play (again, because time is short). The story is excellent and I would reinforce it with the song and actions – I can see the children will go out singing this! The prayer is great for pre-schoolers as they can be involved and it keys into their natural curiosity.

Former primary school teacher, Barbara, has been helping to run a carer-and-toddler group once a week for the past nine years. The room is set out with various activities for the 60 or more children who come and there is a group singing session to round off the morning.

Barbara's choice

We'd use the Song time and the songs from Extra time too. Maybe the story and the rhyme, though very few of our children are used to listening to a story in a group. The game and making ideas would need to be prepared beforehand and have adult help, but I'd like to try these. Talking with the adults could be interesting too.

Mandy has a small group of 2- to 6-year-olds in her Sunday morning club and up to 20 attending her midweek outreach group, which focuses on music and dance.

Mandy's choices

For Sunday morning club

I like the focused Play time, though we would have to reduce the time allowed for this. Making time supports the story and I like using easy-access junk materials. I love the dramatic interpretation of the story. The song would be easy to do. We wouldn't have time for a game or rhyme, but I like the responsive child-inclusive prayer. Unfortunately, I don't get much chance to talk to parents, but the activity page would be a way of sharing with them.

For midweek music group

We don't usually share stories but this would be fun and not at all threatening to non-church adults. I'd follow up with the rhyme or the song. We often enjoy chanting rhymes and I liked the use of a familiar tune, with words that fit well. We don't have play or craft, but I would set up the fishing game for the children to play while we have an informal coffee-and-chat at the end.

Jesus loves children

Luke 18: 15–17

Play time

no limit

Welcome

Make a special point of welcoming everyone as they come through the door. Have a selection of toys available and ask them what they would like to play with. Then tell them that you are really pleased to see them and that you hope they will enjoy themselves.

Welcome banner

You will need: a length of wallpaper, glue, sticky shapes, scraps of gift wrap, collage scraps.

In one corner of your room roll out a length of wallpaper and write on the back the word 'Welcome' in large outline letters. Invite every child to come and stick some sticky shapes, or squares of shiny gift wrap on to the letters. The result will be a glittery banner that you can display in your entrance.

Hospitality

You will need: play food and toy tea set.

Set out a selection of play food and plastic cups and plates. Ask the children to help you lay the table and have a pretend tea party. Talk about how you make friends feel welcome when they come to your home and ask the children what they do in their house, eg open the door with a welcoming smile, hang up their coat, offer to share toys, give them a drink and biscuit. Explain that in the story we will hear how Jesus gave some people a warm welcome.

Run, walk, stop

You will need: three paper circles in green, orange and red.

Play this informal game together. Hold up the green circle: everyone runs around. Hold up the orange: everyone walks. Hold up red: everyone must stop and welcome someone in a particular way, eg say 'hello' to as many different people as possible, shake hands with lots of people, say 'I'm pleased to see you!' to everyone, find out as many names as you can.

Game time

 per game: 1 min

One-minute challenge

Sit in a big circle and ask a leader to go round the whole group saying welcome or hello to every child and adult one by one. Did they manage to speak to everyone in one minute; is there someone who thinks that they could do it faster? (If you have a small group, choose a different time limit.) Let one or two children have a go and see how far they get round the circle in one minute. It doesn't take long to smile at people and say 'hello' or 'welcome', but sometimes we're so busy playing or chatting that we forget to do this. Today we're going to hear how, even though Jesus was very busy, he took the time to give some children a very special welcome.

Making time

 10 mins

Welcome cards

You will need: ovals of card, eye, nose and mouth shapes, black, brown, yellow and orange wool, glue, A4 sheets of thin card, hole punch, ribbon.

Give each child an oval of card and ask them to make a picture of their face. Have ready some eye shapes in blue, green and

brown and some noses and mouths to choose from. Help the children to stick these on to the card, and then add some wool for hair. Fix the face onto a piece of thin A4 card and write the child's name and a welcome greeting underneath, eg 'Tom says "Welcome!"' Punch two holes in the top of the card and thread a piece of ribbon through. Let the children take the welcome signs home to hang up.

Story time

 5 mins

Jesus loves children

*Invite everyone to act out the story with you. Ask the adults to play the part of the parents; the children, obviously can be the children; your co-leaders, Jesus' followers and someone should play the part of Jesus. Group 'parents and children' at one end of the room and walk across the room, as you tell the story. Prompt the various groups to join in and repeat the key phrases (shown in **bold** type).*

One very sunny morning lots of children were excited. When they woke up, their mums and dads said, 'Let's go and see Jesus!' Let's pretend that we're just waking up and someone says that to us. '**Let's go and see Jesus today!**'

The children got dressed very quickly and they ate their breakfast super-fast because they were so excited. 'We're going to see Jesus, we're going to see Jesus!' they said. (*Mime getting dressed and eating breakfast; chant, '**We're going to see Jesus!**'*)

They left their houses and skipped happily down the road. (*Start walking.*) They walked and walked until… they could see Jesus and his friends. '**We're going to see Jesus!**' they chattered happily. But do you know, when they got close to Jesus, his friends came over and said, '**Sorry, you can't see Jesus. He's much too busy to speak to you.**' (*Leaders stop the group and say this.*)

How do you think the children felt? That's right! They felt very sad and disappointed because they were really looking forward to seeing Jesus. They turned round and started to walk home.

But do you know what happened next? Jesus saw them and he shouted out to them. '**Stop! Let the children come and see me! I really want to see them!**'

And so, all the mums and dads and children went back to see Jesus. '**We're going to see Jesus!**' they all laughed.

Jesus put his hand on every child's head and said, 'God bless you!' They were so happy to see Jesus. And Jesus was so happy to see them!

This time, when it was time for the children to go home, they felt really happy. They knew that Jesus loved them and thought that they were important.

Rhyme time

Welcome!
Use the following words to welcome all the children and then repeat the words several times so that everyone can join in. Try to look at a different person each time you say the word 'welcome'.

Welcome, welcome, welcome!
It's good to see you today.
We're glad you've come to our group.
We hope you want to play.

Welcome, welcome, welcome!
Jesus wants to welcome you.
He's pleased you've come to see us
And we feel the same way too.

Also:

'Come to me', *LSS* p54
'Shall we go to Jesus?' *LSS* p54

Song time

We're with Jesus!
Use the song 'He's got the whole wide world in his hands' (JU p60), and insert the children's own names into the second and third lines. Explain that 'he' is Jesus and remind the children of how much he wanted to spend time with children.

For example:

He's got the whole world in his hands,
He's got *Ben and Amy* in his hands,
He's got *Tom, Zack and Claire*
    in his hands,
He's got the whole world in his hands.

Also:

'Jesus loves us', *LACH* p43

'People brought children to Jesus', *KS* 280
'Whether you're one', *KS* 384
'This is a song for the children', *KS* 340
'Jesus' love is very wonderful', *JU* p14
'Everyone matters to Jesus', *JU* p2
'Jesus, Jesus, here I am', *JU* p96

Pray time

All of us
Encourage the children to shout out 'Thank you, Jesus!' every time they hear the words 'so we say...'

Whether we're tall or only small,
Jesus welcomes us into his family,
so we say...
Thank you, Jesus!

Whether we're one or one hundred and one,
Jesus welcomes us into his family,
so we say...
Thank you, Jesus!

Whether we crawl or toddle or run,
Jesus welcomes us into his family,
so we say...
Thank you, Jesus!

Whether we're dark, brown-haired, auburn or fair,
Jesus welcomes us into
his family,
so we say...
Thank you, Jesus!

Thank you, Jesus, that you welcome us all into your family.

Extra time

•Enlarge picture 318 or 319 of Jesus and the children from *How to Cheat at Visual Aids! The Collection*, published by SU, ISBN 1 85999 5000 4, to make a colouring sheet.

•Use some of the activities on the Welcome time pages (92 and 93). Each *Tiddlywinks* Big Book has more ideas.

•'Superstar', *LACH* p83

•Read *I Love You*, by Leena Lane, God and Me series, published by SU, ISBN 1 85999 537 3.

Adults too

Church-based groups might consider inviting the church minister to come along and extend a warm welcome to everyone, inviting them to the next all-age service. Why not print out some small invitation cards? Do you have any other groups that would appeal to the parents and carers that come to your group, perhaps an Alpha course or, on a social level, a badminton group or similar? Print the details of all your church activities on the reverse of your invitation card so that people know what else the church offers besides the Tiddlywinks group.

Top tip

Think about what it would be like to come to your group for the first time. Would you know whom to approach first? Do you have a desk where everyone signs in? (This would be good practice from a safety perspective so that you know who is in the building.) Many large groups benefit from having extra adults around who can chat to new people and help out with craft activities and refreshments. Parents or carers with more than one child will always value an extra pair of hands as they struggle to feed their youngest, while also helping their toddler with gluing and sticking. Helpers who have older children can be great as they have a wealth of parenting experience to draw on.

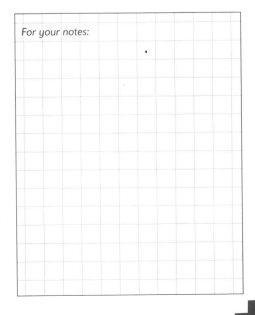

ACTIVITY PAGE:
The photocopiable activity page for this outline is on page 18

For your notes:

15

The lost sheep

Luke 15: 1–7

Play time

no limit

Farm animals
You will need: play farm, toy animals.

Have a selection of toys laid out for when the children first arrive. If possible, include a farmyard with animals. Spend some time talking about what the animals eat and who looks after them. Discuss the noises that different animals make. Group the animals according to species, size or colour. Talk about farmers and shepherds, and how they look after their animals. Make sure that all the children know what a shepherd is and what the job involves. Count the number of animals of each type. Explain that in the story we will hear about a shepherd who counted his one hundred sheep.

Missing pieces!
You will need: jigsaw puzzles.

Set out one or two simple jigsaw puzzles. Remove one piece from each puzzle before your session and hide it somewhere near. (Don't forget where it is!) Help those children who come to the puzzle table to put together one of the pictures. When they discover that there is a piece missing, ask them to help you to look for it. Once the piece is found and put into the picture, make a point of thanking that child and telling the group how clever they were to find the missing piece.

Lost and found
You will need: 'lost property' list.

Interrupt your Play time to explain that you have lost some important things and ask that, if anyone finds them, they should give them back to you. Show the children the list of lost property with a picture clue for each one, for example, a bunch of keys, a glove, a teddy, a packet of wet-wipes and a notebook. You'll probably find that older pre-schoolers will enjoy looking for the missing objects while the toddlers remain absorbed in their own activities. Tick off each item as it is found.

Game time

3-5 mins per game

Getting warmer
You will need: a soft toy sheep.

Send one child out of the room with a helper or their parent/carer. Hide your sheep somewhere in the room for them to find. When they return, explain that you will all help them to find the toy by telling them when they are close to it ('getting warmer', 'warm' or 'hot') or in the wrong place ('getting colder' or 'cold'). Demonstrate what you mean – then play!

Hide and seek
You will need: nine large sheets of paper with ten sheep drawn on each; one sheet with nine sheep; one odd sheep, Blu-tack.

Put the groups of sheep around the room, church or garden and hide the single sheep. Send the children off (each with an adult) to gather in the flock. Bring them all together and count them to discover that one is missing: find it!

Making time

10 mins

Sheep masks
You will need: mask shapes from page 19 copied or mounted on card, PVA glue, cotton wool, crayons, hole punch, hole reinforcements or sticky tape, elastic or thin cane or dowel.

Help the children to colour in their sheep masks, particularly the nose and ears. Spread PVA glue over the sheep's woolly topknot and let the children stick on some cotton wool. Punch a hole in either side. Strengthen the hole with reinforcements or a piece of sticky tape and tie a length of elastic across or tape a handle to the back. Let the children wear their masks to sing 'Baa baa black sheep'. They'll also enjoy suggesting new colours to sing, eg 'Baa baa purple sheep'!

Story time

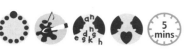

5 mins

The lost sheep
You will need: a toy lamb.

As the story progresses, lead the children round the room, or building, till you 'find' your lost lamb (hidden beforehand). If space is limited, perform the story on the spot using your hands to suggest some of the action. Encourage everyone to join in with the sound effects printed in bold.

I'm a sad shepherd because I've lost my little lamb. He's small and white and very special and I love him very much. Will you come with me and help me to find him? First we must climb up this steep hill, it's really hard work... **(Sigh, phew!)**. Uh oh, here are some sharp prickly bushes; we'll have to be very careful... **(Ooch, ouch!)**. Can you see the little lamb anywhere? No! We'd better keep looking then!

Now we've come to a stream, we'll have to paddle through it... **(Splish, splash!)**. Oh dear, the riverbanks are rather muddy, don't get stuck in the mud will you? **(Squelch, squelch!)**. Can you see the little lamb anywhere? No! We'd better keep looking then!

And here's a field of long grass, let's run through it **(Swish, swish!)**. Oh look! The next bit is downhill, let's run as fast as we can... **(Wheeeee!)**. Can you see the little lamb anywhere? No! We'd better keep looking then!

Do you see those big rocks over there? Shall we go and take a closer look? We'd better go quietly on tiptoe, just in case

there are any wild animals about!...
(Shhh, shhh!). Did you hear something just then? I thought I heard a little lamb! Let's all listen! *(Baa, baa!)* Oh look, here's the little lamb, he's got his foot stuck, let's rescue him. Hooray, he's free! I'll pop him inside my coat and we'll take him back home. Can you remember the journey?

First we must go back over the rocks, climb back up the hill *(Sigh, phew!)*, through the long grass *(Swish, swish)* carefully over the muddy riverbank... *(Squelch, squelch!)*, through the river... *(Splish, splash!)*, here are the prickly bushes... *(Ooch, ouch!)*. Nearly there, let's just run down this last hill *(Wheeeee!)* and we're home at last! Hooray!

Thank you for helping me to find my very precious lamb. Now let's have a rest and a drink and biscuit!

Rhyme time

Lost little sheep
All pretend to be the little lost sheep while one of the group leaders or a confident child is the shepherd looking for you. The words can also be sung to the tune of 'Baa baa black sheep'.

Baa baa little sheep
    who's lost on the hill,
The shepherd will find you,
    yes he will!
He looks all night, he looks all day,
He's looking for the little lamb
    who's lost his way!

Baa baa little sheep
    who's lost his own way,
The shepherd has found you,
    hip hip hooray!
He really cares for you, he loves you,
And Jesus really loves us
    in the same way too.

One little sheep
One little sheep, she went to play,
One little sheep, she went away.
The good, kind shepherd searched all day.
He found his sheep and he said, 'Hooray!'

Song time

Loving shepherd
Sing the following words to the tune of 'Little Bo Peep':

Loving shepherd has lost his lamb
And doesn't know where to find it,
He searches all night with all his might
And praises God when he finds it.

Also:

'Jesus' love is very wonderful', *JU* p14
'Whether you're one', *KS* 384
'One, two, three Jesus loves me!', *KS* 274

Pray time

Look at us!
You will need: paper people shapes, crayons, PVA glue, large poster paper.

Give each child a very simple paper person shape. Ask them to draw their own smiley face on the figure and add some hair and clothes. Little ones will simply colour the whole figure one colour, but that's great too! Ask the adults to add the children's names and then glue all the figures on to a large piece of paper, to make a happy crowd. Point to each figure in turn as you pray:

Thank you Jesus that you love us just as much as the shepherd loved his lost sheep. Thank you that you know each one of us by name, and each member of our family too. Thank you that you love *Jade* and *Tom*, *Sami* and *Charlotte*, etc.

Extra time

•Wear sheep masks and sing or say 'Little Bo Peep' and 'Mary had a little lamb'.

•Find more sheep rhymes in *Let's Sing and Shout!* pages 58–60, published by SU, ISBN 1 85999263 3.

•Pictures 48,49 and 78–82 from the New Testament section of *How to Cheat at Visual Aids*, The Collection, published by SU, ISBN 1 8999500 4, can be used to make colouring sheets or visual aids.

Adults too

A meditation using Psalm 23.
Read the words slowly, over some lilting background music. With the music still playing, make these points:

A shepherd leads the way and directs the flock; he doesn't want even a single lamb to get left behind. A shepherd cares for injured sheep and protects his flock from danger. He knows each of his sheep by name and recognises when one is missing. He takes his sheep to nourishing pastures and refreshing streams. Jesus knows and cares about us and about each member of our family in just the same way. He wants to protect us from danger and satisfy our needs. We might think that Jesus wouldn't miss us if we were to go our own way, but he would.

Like the shepherd, he knows each one of us by name and recognises when even a single one of us is missing, hurt, in need or unhappy.

Top tips

•This might be an appropriate week to display the contents of your lost property box and reunite items with their owners!

•**Be safe!** If you are going beyond your normal meeting area when playing 'seeking' games, make sure each child is teamed with an adult and that all doors leading outside are firmly shut.

•Check your records to see if there are people you have lost touch with. What could you do to invite them back, or to encourage them to be involved in something else your church offers?

> **ACTIVITY PAGE:**
> The photocopiable activity page for this outline is on page 19.
> Copy this onto thin card.

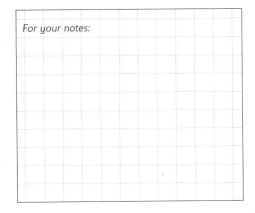

For your notes:

Jesus loves children.

Here is Jesus – but where are the children?
Draw lots of children coming to see him!

Luke 18:
15-17

My
name

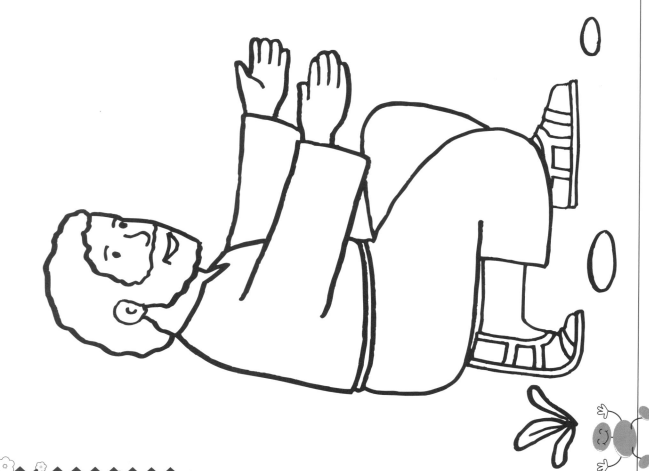

Jesus loves us, just as a shepherd loves his sheep.

My name

Use this page to make a sheep mask. Photocopy the mask onto thin card. Cut it out. Colour in the face and stick cotton wool to the woolly top-knot. Punch a hole on either side of the mask, then tie a length of elastic to fit. Or tape a stick to the reverse side to make a handle for holding the mask.

Luke 15: 1–7

3 Jesus loves me
Jairus' daughter

Mark 5: 21–43

Play time

no limit

Doll's hospital
You will need: toys, toys for doll's hospital, toy doctor's bag and dressing-up clothes (optional).

Have a selection of bricks, cars, puzzles and other toys laid out for when the children first arrive. Turn one corner of your room into a doll's hospital with dolls, teddies, blankets, pillows, bandages and a box of plasters. Try to ensure that all the children have the chance to visit this corner before Story time.

Fever pitch
You will need: a thermometer or fever strip.

Jairus' daughter probably had a high fever. Use a thermometer or a fever strip to take the children's temperatures. Explain how the thermometer tells us when someone is too hot or too cold. It can be a good idea to practise taking temperatures when children are healthy so that they don't make a fuss when they are poorly. In this instance the activity will need close adult supervision, since many thermometers are made of glass and contain mercury. Don't put the thermometer in the children's mouths, as this might spread germs, but tuck it under their armpits.

Traffic jam
Use a selection of toy cars and a toy ambulance to show how ambulances are able to overtake the other traffic. Line up cars to make traffic jams and 'drive' the ambulances past them. Talk about when and why people might need an ambulance. Explain that the little girl in our story was very poorly, but in those days there were no ambulances.

Keep fit
Do some simple exercises: stretching up and out to the side, shaking arms from shoulders and wrists, bending elbows, touching toes, standing on tiptoe, bending knees, jogging on the spot, leg shaking.

Play some lively music while you exercise.

Game time

5 mins

Feely bag
You will need: a toy doctor's set, pillow case.

Empty a toy doctor's bag into a pillowcase (eg stethoscope, tweezers, notepad, bandages, toy scissors). Invite individual children to come up, feel one of the items and guess what it is. Take the item out of the bag to see if the child is right and then talk about how it is used.

Mime time
Ask an adult to mime various simple ailments for the children to guess what's wrong, eg: falling over and bumping your knee, removing a splinter, coughing and sneezing with a bad cold, limping with a blister on your foot, a bad headache. Discuss how feeling ill makes people feel miserable and let the children talk about times when they've felt ill.

Making time

10 mins

Into bed!
You will need: Activity page 24 copied on to card for each child, crayons, scissors, PVA glue.

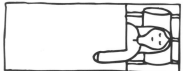

Cut out the bed and pictures of Jairus' poorly/healthy daughter. Let the children work with their carers to colour the bed and the girl. Then, glue the two sides of the girl together to make a reversible figure. Fold over the bed covers and glue down the tabs so that Jairus' daughter can be slotted into the bed.

Story time

5 mins

Jesus helps and heals
*Make a large scale example of the model from Activity page 24 as a visual aid. Begin with Jairus' daughter looking poorly; turn her over at the point in the story when Jesus heals her. Encourage the children to join in saying, 'very, very poorly' after you. Omit the section from ** to *** if you want a shorter story.*

Jairus and his wife stood beside their little daughter's bed. She was hot and sticky and **very, very poorly.**

'Whatever can we do?' asked Jairus. 'She has been ill for days. The doctors haven't been able to help her.' They hated seeing their little girl lying there looking **very, very poorly,** not eating, drinking or speaking.

'Jesus cares about people who are **very, very poorly.**' said Jairus' wife. 'Let's ask him to come and see our daughter.'

So, Jairus rushed off to town to look for Jesus. He ran as fast as he could and when he finally found Jesus he was out of breath. 'Jesus, Jesus!' he panted. 'Please come at once! My little daughter is **very, very poorly.** We need your help!'

Jesus said, 'Yes, I'll come right now.' ** But the crowds of people delayed them because they also wanted Jesus' help. 'Please, please come quickly,' said Jairus. 'My daughter really is **very, very poorly.** Please come before it's too late.'

Just then one of Jairus' servants came rushing down the street, 'Don't bother Jesus any more!' he said. 'No one can help your little girl now.' Two big tears rolled down Jairus' sad face.

'Don't worry, Jairus,' said Jesus kindly. 'Just trust me and she will get well.'

When Jairus took Jesus into his home everyone was sobbing and crying because they all loved the little girl very much. ***

Jesus went and stood by the little girl's bed.

Jesus took hold of her hand and said softly, 'Get up my child!' Instantly her white cheeks became a healthy pink and she sat up and smiled. 'Hello!' she said looking around. 'What happened? I was **very, very poorly,** but now I feel really, really well. Thank you!'

'And now,' said Jesus, 'I think that you should give her something to eat!'

And that's just what they did. Jesus went away, feeling pleased that the little girl was better now. Jesus always cares about people who are **very, very poorly.**

Rhyme time

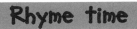

Quick, Jesus!
Emphasise the beat as you chant this story rhyme. Why not invite children to mime the parts.

Jairus' daughter was very, very sick,
So he called for Jesus very, very quick.
'It's urgent!' said Jairus.
　'Come now, don't wait!'
But his servant said,
　'Sorry, it's already too late!'

Jesus replied 'Don't worry, believe in me.
Your daughter will get better,
　just wait and see!'
At Jairus' home the people were weeping.
'She'll be fine!' said Jesus.
　'She's only sleeping!'

He went to her bed and took her
　by the hand,
'Little girl, get up, I'll help you to stand.'
The little girl smiled and got out of bed.
'What a wonderful miracle!'
　the people said.

Song time

Sing our thanks
Focus on being well and on Jesus' love for us (whether well or ill) with some happy songs. Sing to 'Thank you, Lord, for this fine day' (JP 232).

Thank you, Lord,

for health and strength, *(x 3)*
Thank you, thank you, Lord.

Create more verses, using ideas from the children wherever possible. You could try:

Thank you, Lord, for feeling well…

Thank you, Lord, for doctors and nurses…

Thank you, Lord, for loving us…

Also:

'Jesus' hands were kind hands', *KS* 194
'Jesus' love is very wonderful', JR p14
'The body song', *JR* p62
'Jairus and Jesus', *LACH* p52

Pray time

Thank you, Lord!
Help the group to rejoice in the movements of their healthy bodies by fitting appropriate actions to this prayer. Encourage the children to join in with the response: 'Thank you, Lord'.

For arms that swing and hands that clap,
Thank you, Lord!

For feet that stamp and toes that tap,
Thank you, Lord!

For legs that jump and run and walk,
Thank you, Lord!

For heads that nod and mouths that talk,
Thank you, Lord!

Because we can crouch down low then jump up high,
Thank you, Lord!

Because we can stand on tiptoe and reach for the sky,
Thank you, Lord!

For giving us bodies that bend and stretch and move,
Thank you, Lord!

Extra time

•Read: *Topsy and Tim Go to the Doctor,* by Jean and Gareth Adamson, published by Ladybird, ISBN 1 90435129 8 or *Going to the Doctor* from the series 'First experiences', published by Usborne, ISBN 0 74604117 9.

•Say or act out 'Miss Polly had a dolly who was sick, sick, sick'.

Adults too

•Make a group collage of magazine pictures showing people running, walking, jumping, playing etc. Add the caption, 'Thank you, God, for good health.'

Point out that when Jairus' daughter was ill he turned directly to Jesus. Jesus wants us to go to him with all our needs. He loves us and each member of our family very much and we can take our concerns to him. If there are a large number of non-church families in your group, you might like to explain that you believe in the power of prayer and regularly pray for people who are ill or in hospital. Ask the adults if there is anyone special that they would like you to pray for now or in your personal prayers.

Update your notice board with health information, particularly on issues of concern which are currently in the news. Obtain leaflets from your local clinic, health centre or doctors' surgery.

Top tip

Keep a register so that you can tell if a child or their carer has been ill or unable to attend. Some parents can feel (and be) very isolated when they are housebound with young children who are suffering childhood ailments, especially if they live a long way from their family. You could check whether they need medicine collecting or loan a few videos to amuse the invalid. These are tangible ways of showing Christian care.

ACTIVITY PAGE:
The photocopiable activity page for this outline is on page 24.
Copy this onto thin card.

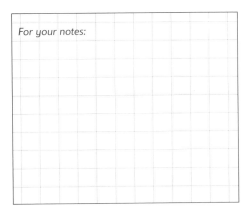

For your notes:

21

4 Jesus loves me
The kind traveller

Luke 10: 25–32

Play time

   no limit

Travel and transport
You will need: toy vehicles.

In your free play area, include a variety of toy cars, planes, boats, tractors, etc and discuss all the different ways the children can think of travelling. Which vehicles are fast and which are slow? Old or new? Big or small?

Tail on the donkey
You will need: a big picture of a donkey without a tail, a tail on a separate piece of card with a piece of Blu-tack on the back.

Ask the children, one at a time, to close their eyes tightly: let them try to fix the tail on to the right place on the donkey. Have this activity available during your Play time, so that children can come over and have a go. Young children don't generally have the patience to watch many other children take their turn. Explain that in today's story a man was offered a ride on a donkey.

Bikes, trikes and ride-ons
You will need: ride-ons, cones or chairs.

If you have plenty of space and can section off one end of your room, or if you can go outside, have a selection of ride-on toys for the children to play with. Set out cones or a row of chairs for the children to ride round and ask a leader to direct the traffic. Older pre-schoolers will enjoy obeying hand signals, eg: a beckoning hand means keep going, one hand up means stop and one blast on a whistle means change direction.

Alternatively, set out a row of chairs to make a bus or train and imagine going on a special journey, pack a play-food picnic and take some cuddly toy friends. Give out paper tickets and appoint a conductor to check them.

Game time

4 mins per game

Car races
You will need: toy cars, chalk or string.

Mark two lines on the floor with chalk or string and let the children race small cars to the finishing line. Explain that today's story is about a man a long time ago, who was making a journey. There were no cars, trains or planes then, so how does the group think he travelled?

Follow that car

Play 'Follow my leader', with the leader at the front miming different types of transport and the children following behind, copying the action and the sound effect, eg ambulance – steering wheel and 'nee-nah' sound effect; plane – arms out flying and humming noise; walking – walking around swinging arms.

Making time

5 mins **or no limit**

Helping hands
You will need: poster paint, paintbrushes, sheets of thin card, paper, backing paper, clean-up equipment.

Help the children to make a set of handprints on a folded piece of A4 card. Lightly paint each child's hand with poster paint and then press their hand down on to the card. This gives a less smudgy and more detailed print than dipping hands into the paint. Once the prints are dry, add the date and a caption like, 'Sam's helping hands!' Let the children take the cards home to display.

Let the children make a second set of prints, this time on paper. Cut them out and stick them all on to a large sheet of backing paper under the heading, 'Thank you, Lord, for helping hands.'

Story time

10 mins

The kind traveller
You will need: cuddly toys or Duplo figures (optional).

This story loosely fits the tune of 'The wheels on the bus'. As they recognise the pattern, the children should be able to join in with the repeated phrases. If you want the parents and carers to join in with the singing, display the words on an OHP or similar. You could use toys to represent all the characters in the story, or let a child come out to the front to play each role.

A man was walking out of town,
    out of town, out of town,
A man was walking out of town,
    here he comes.
Some robbers were looking out for him
    out for him, out for him,
Some robbers were looking out for him,
    here they come.
They took his money and kicked him hard,
    kicked him hard, kicked him hard.
They took his money and kicked him hard,
    how unkind.
Now a holy man came walking past,
    walking past, walking past,
Now a holy man came walking past,
    here he comes.
He shook his head saying 'I can't stop!
    I can't stop! I can't stop!'
He shook his head saying 'I can't stop!'
    Walked on by.
And then a rich man came walking past,
    walking past, walking past,
And then a rich man came walking past,
    here he comes.
He saw the poor man and passed on by,
    passed on by, passed on by.
He saw the poor man and passed on by,
    there he goes.

Another traveller came riding along,
   riding along, riding along,
Another traveller came riding along,
   here he comes.
He saw the hurt man and stopped to help,
   stopped to help, stopped to help,
He saw the hurt man and stopped to help,
   oh how kind.
He bandaged him up and gave him a ride,
   gave him a ride, gave him a ride,
He bandaged him up and gave him a ride.
   Clippety, clippety, clop.
The traveller took the man to an inn,
   man to an inn, man to an inn,
The traveller took the man to an inn
   to get well.
The traveller paid with silver coins,
   silver coins, silver coins,
The traveller paid with silver coins
   for his care.
The traveller was the kindest man,
   kindest man, kindest man,
The traveller was the kindest man,
   he stopped to help.

Rhyme time

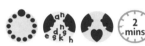

Teddy's bad head
My furry teddy has fallen out of bed,
And now he's got a bump
   on his furry forehead,
I bandaged him quite tightly,
   just as Mummy said,
And tucked him back into
   my cosy, warm bed.

Helping friends
Sit in a circle for this action rhyme.

If I help you, *(Offer right hand to person next to you.)*
And you help me, *(Offer left hand to person next to you and join hands.)*
Oh how happy we will be,
Helping others every day, *(Still holding hands, lift them up and down.)*
In our work and in our play.

Song time

Hands and feet
Sing the following words to the tune, 'Do you know the muffin man?'

Do you have two helping hands,

two helping hands, two helping hands?
Do you have two helping hands?
   It's good to help our friends!

Yes I have two helping hands,
   two helping hands, two helping hands!
Yes I have two helping hands!
   I like to help my friends!

Do you have two willing feet,
   two willing feet, two willing feet?
Do you have two willing feet?
   It's good to help our friends!

Yes I have two willing feet,
   two willing feet, two willing feet!
Yes I have two willing feet,
   I like to help my friends.

Also:

'Jesus hands were kind hands' *KS* 194
'Two little eyes to look to God' *KS* 345

Pray time

Being a helper
Talk about the kind traveller and how he stopped to help the man. Ask the children what kind of things they do to help their friends and family. Weave their ideas into a prayer and invite them to join in with the response.

When mum is busy with lots to do,
Help me to use my helping hands.

When there's shopping to put away,
Help me to use my helping hands.

When there are toys to be tidied up,
Help me to use my helping hands.

When Dad's keys need to be found,
Help me to use my helping hands.

When someone needs a little extra help,
Help me to use my helping hands.

Extra time

•A complete set of photocopiable pictures to illustrate this story can be found in *How to Cheat at Visual Aids, The Collection*, published by SU, ISBN 1 85999 500 4.

•The 'medical' theme of this story is explored in *Tiddlywinks: The Big Red Book*, published by SU, ISBN 1 85999658 2.

•Enjoy *The Good Samaritan pop-up book*, by Mellentin and Wood, published by SU, ISBN 1 85999259 5.

Adults too

The story, better known as 'The good Samaritan', challenges our assumptions and prejudices. Those who listened to Jesus' story would not have expected a Samaritan to stop and help since they were traditional enemies of the Israelites. A modern equivalent might be that a football fan is robbed and beaten up after a match and left lying by the road. The team chaplain doesn't stop to help, the team doctor doesn't stop to help, but a fan of the rival team and traditional arch enemy stops to help the injured fan. He lends him his coat and takes him to hospital by taxi, at his own expense.

Chat about the story with the parents and carers and try to come up with some other modern equivalents.

Top tip

Do you give the children and adults opportunities to be helpful during your sessions? Involve everyone in genuine tasks, such as putting toys away (use large, labelled toy boxes, so that everyone knows where things belong), handing biscuits round, collecting empty cups. It's a good idea to clear up before you have Story time and singing so that there are no toys around to distract the children.

ACTIVITY PAGE:
The photocopiable activity page for this outline is on page 25.
Copy this onto thin card.

For your notes:

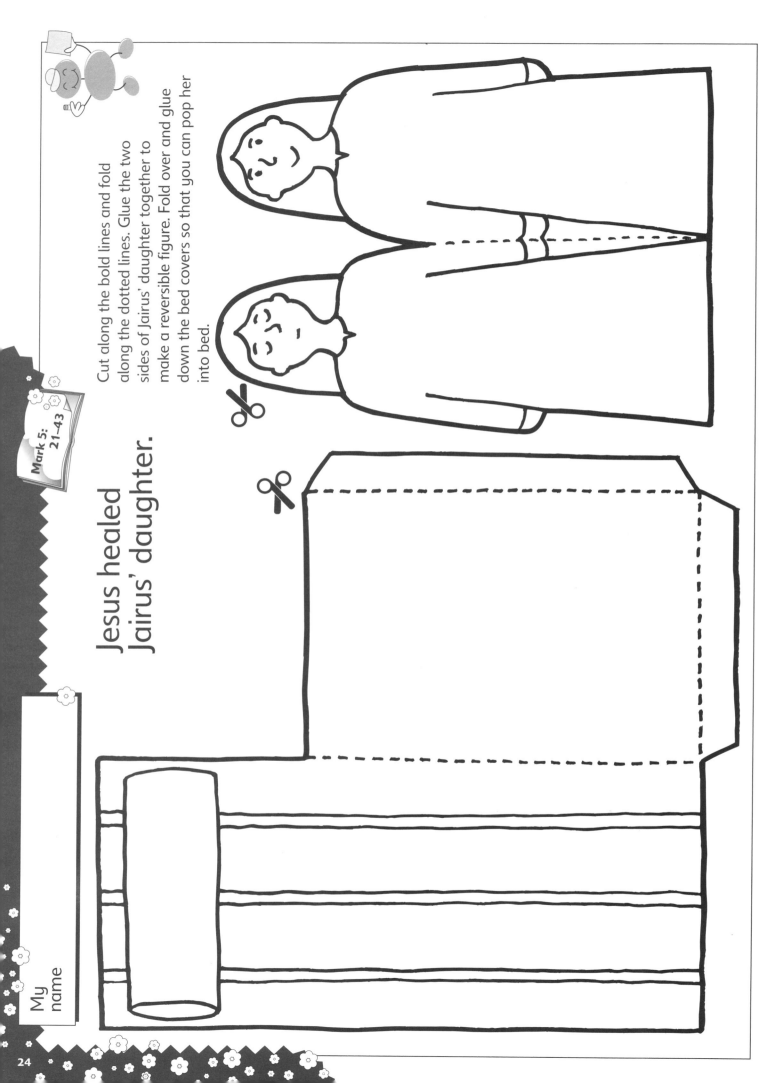

Mark 5: 21–43

Jesus healed Jairus' daughter.

Cut along the bold lines and fold along the dotted lines. Glue the two sides of Jairus' daughter together to make a reversible figure. Fold over and glue down the bed covers so that you can pop her into bed.

My name

Help the kind traveller to
help the man who is hurt.

Colour and cut out the sections. Ask a grown-up to help you
put the model together, using paper fasteners.
Fix the legs on the donkey.
Put the hurt man on the donkey's back.

My
name

Luke 10:
25–37

25

The son who went away

Luke 15: 11–32

Play time

no limit

Cut and stick

You will need: catalogues, round-ended scissors, glue sticks, paper.

Among your free play activities include a table with some scissors and a selection of catalogues for the children to cut out pictures of things that they might like to have. Toy catalogues will be most popular! Help the children to stick all the pictures that they cut out on to a sheet of paper to take home. Children love cutting and sticking, and this activity will help them to develop their hand-eye coordination. Today's story is about a young man who spent a lot of money very quickly.

Homes and families

You will need: Duplo bricks or similar and play people.

Build houses out of bricks and fill them with play people. Act out scenes in which play people leave home to go to school, to work or on holiday, while the other play people wave 'Goodbye!' In the story someone leaves home to go on a long trip.

Drawing corner

You will need: family photos, paper house shapes, crayons.

Bring in some family photos to show the children, and then chat to them about their own families. Give out the paper houses and let the children draw on their family. For children who come from complex family structures, ask them to draw the people who live in the same house as them. Talk about how all families are special to God, whatever size or shape, however big or small. God wants us to love and look after each member of our family.

Story corner

Read about some special father–son relationships in *Guess how much I love you* by Sam McBratney, published by Walker Books, ISBN 0 7445 3224 8, or *Little Bear Stories*, published by Walker Books, ISBN 0 7445 8154 0.

Game time

5 mins

Suitcase

You will need: a suitcase packed with ten items you might take on a trip.

Show the children each item in your suitcase. Talk about what you have packed and why. Close the suitcase and ask the children if they can name all of the things that were inside from memory.

Farewell

Make up some pretend conversations and ask the children to guess who you are saying 'Goodbye!' to in each one, eg: 'Goodbye, have a nice day at work, see you later!' (parent)

In the story we're going to hear about a father who was very sad when he had to say 'Goodbye!' to his son who went away on a long trip.

Making time

5 mins

Finger fun

You will need: a set of finger puppets from page 30 copied on to thin card and cut out for each child, crayons.

Have ready a selection of crayons so that the children can colour in their puppets. You will need to decide whether the children can use their puppets as you tell the story, or whether they should be put on one side to play with later.

Story time

5 mins

The son who went away

You will need: 3 finger puppets from activity page 30, purse crammed with toy money.

Show the puppets as you tell the story. Each time the son spends money, take some from the purse – until there is nothing left.

There was once a father who loved his son very much. When the son was old enough he went to his father and said, 'Dad give me my share of the family money. I want to leave home!'

This made the father very sad, but he gave the son his money. *(Put a purse in front of son puppet.)*

The son spent all the money very quickly. He went to new places. *(Spend.)* He spent money on expensive food *(Spend.)*, wonderful clothes *(Spend.)* and parties with all his new friends. *(Spend.)*

Soon, he didn't have any money left. *(Shake purse upside-down.)* All his friends left him. He was very lonely and very hungry.

He found a job on a farm – feeding the pigs! *(Introduce pig puppet.)* The son didn't like the job at all. But he was so hungry, he would have been happy to eat the pig's food!

The son said to himself, 'The men who work for my father have plenty to eat, but I'm starving hungry. I'll go home and say to my father, "I'm really sorry." I'm not good enough to be his son, but he might give me a job and some food to eat.'

So the son set off back to his father's house. *(Walk puppet around.)* 'Will my father be cross?' he asked himself. 'Will he tell me to go away?'

What do you think his father did?

Well, his father wasn't cross. He didn't tell his son to go away. He ran to meet him and gave him a great big hug!

'Dad!' said the son. 'I'm sorry. I'm not good enough to be your son, but can I come and work for you?'

The father hugged him again. 'My dear son,' he smiled, 'I'm so pleased that you're back. I thought I'd lost you forever, but now you're back home where you belong. We'll have a big party! I love you so much and I want everyone to know that you are home again!'

And that's just what they did!

Rhyme time

Why not invite two children to play the parts of the son and the father, and ask them to mime the actions as you say the rhyme?

A son took his money
And went far away,
To buy all the things
That he wanted, one day.

His father was sad
That his dear son was gone,
While the son spent his money,
And had lots of fun!

Soon his money was gone,
No food could be had.
He looked after pigs
And was hungry and sad.

He went home to his father
And said, 'I am sorry.'
His father forgave him,
And gave a big party!

Song time

God loves us
Sing-and-echo the following words to the tune 'Frère Jacques'.

Yes, God loves us, yes, God loves us!
Very much, very much.
Thank you God for your love.
Thank you God for your love.
We love you!
We love you!

Father and son
A finger rhyme to the tune of 'Here we go round the mulberry bush'. Use one thumb to be each character.

This is the father who loves his son,
Loves his son, loves his son,
This is the father who loves his son,
In the story that Jesus told.

This is the son who pleases himself…

This is the son who's sorry now…

This is the father who welcomes his son…
Also:

'God loves you and I love you', *KS 80* (first verse and chorus only)
'One, two, three, Jesus loves me', *KS* 274

Pray time

Loving God
Explain that you are going to say thank you to God for loving each person in the room just as much as the father loved the son in the story. Say the prayer a couple of times to give the children plenty of opportunity to join in with the actions.

Clap, clap, clap my hands to say
     thank you God for loving me.
Stamp, stamp, stamp my feet to say
     thank you God for loving me.
Wave, wave, wave my arms to say
     thank you God for loving me.
Jump, jump, jump up and down to say
     thank you God for loving me.
Kiss, kiss, blow a kiss to say
     thank you God for loving me.

Extra time

•Use the story poem 'The lost son' on page 60 of *Let's All Clap Hands*, published by SU, ISBN 1 85999 528 4.

•Use page 169 of *How to Cheat at Visual Aids! The Collection*, published by SU, ISBN 1 85999 500 4 to retell the story or to make colouring sheets.

•Read *The Prodigal Son* pop-up book, by Mellentin and Wood, published by SU, ISBN 1 85999 258 7.

Adults too

How does this story challenge us as child-carers? Can you imagine yourself forgiving your child, if they were to behave like the son in the story? Sometimes our children try our patience, sometimes they challenge our parenting skills and sometimes they test our ability to forgive. Anyone in a parenting role needs plenty of prayer. Invite the adults to think about their child for a moment while a leader prays that God will bless their young lives and their future hopes.

Alternatively, challenge each parent to spend time every night for a week praying for their child(ren), for their development, their behaviour, their needs and their relationships with others.

Are there local parenting courses you could advertise? Or maybe organise? CARE produces a wide range of resources to support parents including the video-based 'Parent Talk'. Contact CARE for the family, PO Box 448, Cardiff, CF15 7YY.

Top tip

Remember that not every child will be in a loving father–child relationship and not every mum or carer will have a positive experience of being fathered. If some children or adults in your group need extra sensitivity, you might need to talk about God being 'the perfect parent'. Talk about God being the kind of parent you would like to be yourself; loving, caring, kind, generous, everything you could hope for in a perfect parent.

ACTIVITY PAGE:
The photocopiable activity page for this outline is on page 30.
Copy this onto thin card.

For your notes:

6 Jesus loves me
The hole in the roof

Luke 5: 17–26

Play time

no limit

House building
You will need: *free play toys, bricks.*

Set out a selection of free play toys for when the children first arrive and include bricks for the children to build houses. Build at least one house with a flat roof and outside stairs. Set it on one side to show the whole group just before Story time.

Cut and stick
You will need: *shoeboxes, chenille wires, round-ended scissors, paper, glue sticks.*

Make simple Bible houses out of shoeboxes. Turn the box upside down on the table, then glue the lid to the bottom of the box to make a flat roof with a raised wall around the outside. Cut out a door and window. Add some chenille wire figures. Chat about the sorts of homes we live in. Explain that today we will hear about a house in another country. It had a flat roof and stairs that went up the outside of the house and onto the roof. In that country, people would sit, chat and even sleep on the roof! Show the children a picture from a Bible reference book. The Bible story makes very little sense to children who are imagining a house with a sloping roof and chimney!

Music and movement
You will need: *music.*

Play some lively music and encourage the children to hop, skip, jump and dance to the beat. Alternatively, play some action songs and encourage everyone to join in with the words and the actions. The Bible story is about a man who wouldn't have been able to join in with all the actions because his arms and legs didn't work properly, or at least they didn't work at the *beginning* of the story.

Game time

5 mins

Friendly fours
You will need: *old towels, small blankets, dolls, teddies, obstacles.*

Show the children how to lift a doll on a blanket: spread the blanket on the floor, lay the doll in the centre. Have four children take a corner each and lift together. Try carrying the doll in a straight line or around the room: this needs a surprising amount of cooperation and coordination!

Extend the game by setting out a simple obstacle course – perhaps a slalom of chairs, under a low bar on a climbing frame and through a hula hoop held vertically. Can they carry the doll to the end without dropping it? Get the children into teams of four and have a race.

Be safe! Only carry toys in this way, never children!

Making time

10 mins

Fold a Bible house
You will need: *a copy of Activity page 31 copied on to thin card for each child, glue, crayons.*

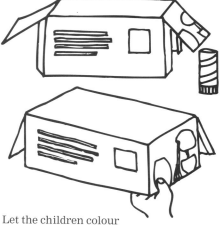

Let the children colour in the houses. Help them to fold the sides

and glue the tabs in place. While you are working, explain that houses like these can be seen in hot countries. They have flat roofs and stairs on the outside of the house so that people can go on to the roof to relax or even to sleep at night. Point out the four friends carrying the man up the stairs on his mat and explain that we'll be hearing more about them in our story. Display the finished houses so that they look like a small town.

Story time

5 mins

Up and down
Tell the story below with the children pointing both index fingers downwards for 'down, down, down', upwards for 'up, up, up' and forwards for 'in, in, in'.

A man was lying **down, down, down** on the ground, feeling sad because he couldn't move. He was feeling **down, down, down** in the dumps because his legs and arms wouldn't work.

Then four kind friends came along and picked him **up, up, up** on his mat saying, 'We're going to take you to see Jesus!'

They came to a very crowded house where Jesus was. They tried to walk **in, in, in** through the door, but the house was so full of people that they couldn't get in.

They tried to climb **in, in, in** through the window, but the house was so crowded that they couldn't squeeze in.

Finally they said, 'Let's climb **up, up, up** the outside stairs and on to the roof.' So that's just what they did.

The four kind friends made a hole in the roof and lowered the man **down, down, down** through the hole, **down, down, down** to see Jesus.

Jesus looked **up, up, up** at the four friends. He saw the hole in the roof and he saw how much the friends believed in him. Jesus smiled at the man and said gently, 'Pick **up, up, up** your bed and walk!' And the man stood **up, up, up** and he was healed.

'Thank you, Jesus!' he said with a huge grin. Then he jumped **up, up, up** and he walked and ran and hopped and skipped **down, down, down** the road and all the way home. And he couldn't stop smiling and laughing because Jesus had healed him and he was SO happy!

Rhyme time

I can move

Say the following rhyme with your group, encouraging all the children to join in with the appropriate actions and the words in bold print. If you have children with disabilities in your group, adapt the words and actions to suit the abilities of your group.

I can stamp my feet and tap my toes.
I can clap my hands and wiggle my nose.
Thank you, Jesus, that I can move!

I can bend in the middle and
   touch the ground.
I can walk on tiptoe without a sound.
Thank you, Jesus, that I can move!

I can hop, skip and jump and run about.
I can stretch up, stretch down and
   stretch out.
Thank you, Jesus, that I can move!

I can swing my arms from side to side,
Stand up straight and tall, or
   reach out wide.
Thank you, Jesus, that I can move!

Song time

The man who couldn't walk

Sing the following words to the tune of, 'Oh the grand old Duke of York.'

Oh the man who couldn't walk,
He had four special friends.
They carried him up to the
   top of the house,
And they lowered him down again.

And Jesus looked up at the friends,
And then he looked down at the man.
'I'm glad you believe in me,' he said,
'I will make you well again.'

Oh the man who couldn't walk,
He had four special friends,
They took him to Jesus, who
   made him well,
And he now can walk again!

Also:

'Head, shoulders, knees and toes'
'One finger, one thumb keep moving'
'I'm a dingle, dangle scarecrow'
'Hokey, cokey'

Pray time

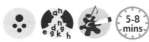

Busy feet

You will need: *a sheet of coloured A4 paper per child, thick wax crayons, scissors.*

Ask each child to place one foot on the paper. Draw round the shoe or foot and cut out the shape. Then ask the children to draw an activity that they like doing, eg running, dancing or kicking a football, on the foot shape. Add a caption, eg 'Ben likes dancing'.

Sit in a circle and thank God for all the things that the children have drawn and for the fun we have moving about. Let the children take their foot pictures home, or stick them all on to backing paper under the title, 'Thank you God that we can move!'

Extra time

• Use pictures 196–202 from *How to Cheat at Visual Aids! The Collection*, published by SU, ISBN 1 85999 500 4, to make colouring sheets and visual aids for the story.

• Play 'Follow my leader' trying out different styles of walking, skipping and jumping around the room.

• Read *Topsy and Tim Make a New Friend*, by Jean and Gareth Adamson, published by Ladybird. ISBN 1 90435 117 4. The story focuses on a new friendship with a little girl in a wheelchair.

• Sing a story song to the tune of 'London Bridge'.

Bits of roof are falling down…
   on to Jesus.

A bed is being lowered down…
   down to Jesus.

A poor lame man is lying down…
   right by Jesus.

Now the man is standing up…
   thanks to Jesus.

Let's all clap hands and shout 'hooray'…
   praise to Jesus.

• Can you name the parts of a leg? Where is the foot, heel, knee, toe, ankle? What are other parts of a leg called?

Adults too

The paralysed man didn't stay on his bed a second longer than he needed: once he was healed, he was up! What does this say to us? Think about what it might mean to be 'walking with Jesus': involving Jesus in our lives, talking to him every day, sharing our joys and worries with him, following in his ways, obeying the rules that God has given us for happy living. Pray that Jesus will help each group member to walk closer to him in the coming week.

Arrange a showing of a video of the life story of Joni Eareckson Tada (Authentic Video & DVD ISBN 1 5640 8027 7), a young woman who was paralysed in an accident and who wasn't healed in the 'get up and walk' sense. The film is still challenging and will stimulate discussion and questions.

Top tip

If you would like to raise some money for a disability charity or if you need to raise money to buy more equipment for your group, why not organise a 'sponsored toddle'? Set an attainable target of a fixed number of laps around a local park and make it into a social event, by including time for a picnic.

ACTIVITY PAGE:
The photocopiable activity page for this outline is on page 31.
Copy this onto thin card.

For your notes:

The father loved his son very much.
God loves us very much.

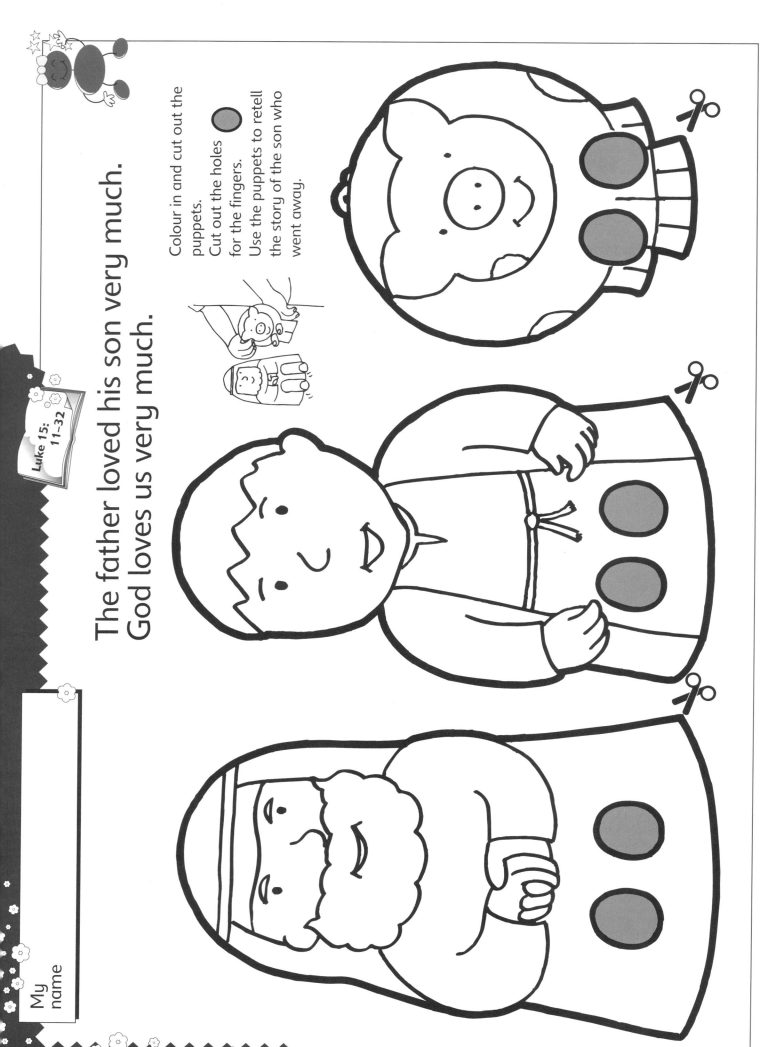

Luke 15: 11–32

Colour in and cut out the puppets.
Cut out the holes for the fingers.
Use the puppets to retell the story of the son who went away.

My name

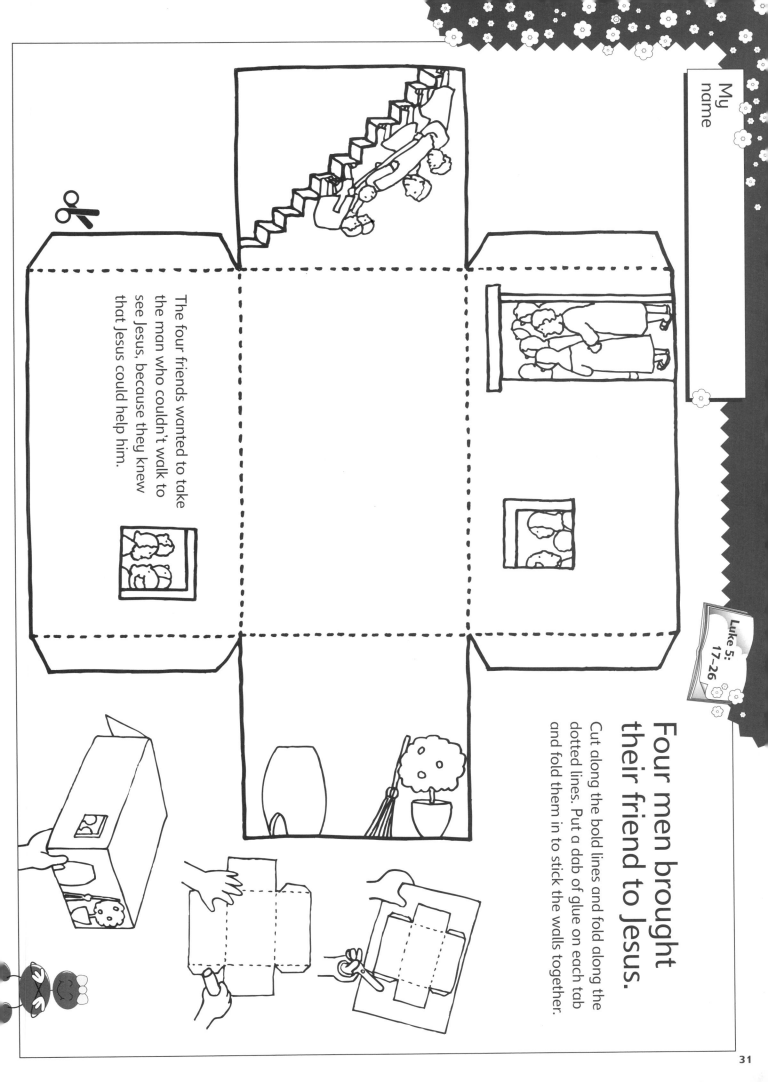

My name

The four friends wanted to take the man who couldn't walk to see Jesus, because they knew that Jesus could help him.

Luke 5: 17-26

Four men brought their friend to Jesus.

Cut along the bold lines and fold along the dotted lines. Put a dab of glue on each tab and fold them in to stick the walls together.

31

Zacchaeus climbs a tree

Luke 19: 1–10

Play time

no limit

Counting coins

You will need: toy money, shop tills, piggy banks, real coins, paper, Blu-tack, wax crayons.

With your free play activities include an area with play money, piggy banks, toy shop, tills, etc. Zacchaeus, in the Bible story, loved money, so give the children the opportunity to count, share out, pile up and put the coins into money boxes. Have some coins, paper and wax crayons for the children to make coin rubbings. Fix the coins to the table with Blu-tack so that they don't move while the children are working.

Leaf and bark rubbing

You will need: paper, wax crayons, Blu-tack, leaves.

On another table have a selection of leaves for the children to make leaf rubbings. Encourage the children to make at least two rubbings, one to take home and one to contribute to the group collage later in the session. While you are working, talk about trees: fruit trees, leafy trees and trees to climb. Explain that the man in today's story climbed a tree.

If you have the opportunity to go outside, take paper and brown wax crayons to make some tree bark rubbings, these can also be used for the group collage in Making time.

Tea party

You will need: a toy tea set, play food.

Set out one corner of your room with play food and a toy tea set. Talk to the children about visiting friends: do they sometimes stay for tea? What is their favourite food? We'll be hearing how Jesus visited Zacchaeus and became his special friend – and they had a meal together.

All friends together

You will need: magazine pictures of people, paper, glue.

Cut out as many pictures of people (of all ages) as you can find from magazines and catalogues. Let the children glue them on to individual or group-sized pieces of paper. Add a caption like: 'Jesus wants us all to be his friends'.

Game time

 5 mins

Guess who?

Ask a leader to describe different members of the group, plus other friends and even pets known to the group, for the children to guess their identity. Use the following format:

'I've got a special friend who's wearing pink trousers. She really likes singing; can anyone guess who it is?'

'I've got a special friend with a black and white fur coat and a waggly tail; can anyone guess who it is?'

Mime time

Explain that you like to do many different things with your friends, then mime some activities for the children to guess what you are doing, eg playing football, building towers, talking on the phone. It's good to have friends to play with and spend time with. Poor Zacchaeus, in the Bible story, had no friends at all.

Making time

 **10 mins**

Climb a tree

You will need: wall paper, brown crayons or paint, PVA glue, leaf rubbings or green paper leaves, enlarged figure of Zacchaeus, sticky shapes, wool.

Draw a simple tree trunk shape on a length of wallpaper. Leave space at the top for leaves. Make sure that there is a branch sticking out sideways where you can place Zacchaeus. Invite a few children to colour or paint the trunk with brown wax crayons or paint. If you have made bark rubbings, you could glue these on to the trunk instead. Guide children to glue the leaf rubbings (if made) or leaf shapes around the top of the tree. Help others to decorate a large outline of Zacchaeus with sticky shapes on his clothes and wool strands for hair.

Story time

 **5 mins**

Zac meets Jesus

Tell the story of Zacchaeus, encouraging the children to join in with actions wherever appropriate.

Zac was always counting money. 'One, two, three gold coins for the Romans and one for me!' Let's help him count… *(Repeat several times.).* Zac collected money from all the people in his town to give to the Roman army. The townspeople didn't like him because he always cheated and took some of the money for himself. Zac had no friends and this made him feel very sad. Can you show me a very sad face?

One day Zac heard that Jesus was coming to his town. Zac really wanted to see Jesus. He ran all the way into town. Let's pretend that we're running fast like Zac.

When Zac arrived, there were crowds of people everywhere. Zac couldn't see a thing. He tried standing on tiptoe like this, but he couldn't see over the heads of the crowd. *(Mime.)* He tried jumping up and down like this, but he still couldn't see anything. *(Mime.)* Then he saw a big tree…

'If I climb into that tree, I'll be able to see everything,' he said. So that's just what he did. Very carefully, he clambered and climbed *(Mime.)* until he was sitting on a branch up above all the people. Let's all sit down and pretend that we are sitting in a big leafy tree.

Soon Jesus and his friends came walking down the street. Everyone cheered and waved, but Zac stayed quietly hidden in his tree. Suddenly, Jesus stopped under the big tree and called out, 'Come down Zacchaeus! I'm coming to your house today.' Zac was so surprised that he nearly fell off his branch. *(Gasp!)*

Zac welcomed Jesus into his house. He was delighted to discover that Jesus wanted to be his special friend. From that moment Zac was a different man. He gave away half of his money to the poor people. He gave back all the money that he'd cheated from people. 'One for you and one for you,' he said. 'I'm so sorry that I took your money.' Let's pretend that we're Zac giving back the money.

Before long Zac had plenty of friends and he told everyone how he had met Jesus and become his friend too.

Rhyme time

Zacchaeus climbs a tree
As a group, make up some actions to use with these words.

Zacchaeus climbed a sycamore tree,
To see if Jesus he could see.
He watched the road both up and down,
Until he saw Jesus come into town.
Jesus stopped under the big tall tree,
And said 'Come down, Zac,
   I'm coming to tea!'
'I'm sorry,' said Zac.
   'I've done things that were bad.'
'I know,' said Jesus,
   'and that makes me sad,
But if you're sorry you can start again
And I want you to be my special friend.'

Song time

Sing these simple verses to the first two lines of 'Jingle bells'. Everyone will

quickly learn the actions!

Clap your hands, clap your hands
   and clap your hands again.
Oh how great it is to know
   that Jesus is your friend!

Stamp your feet, stamp your feet
   and stamp your feet again.
Oh how great it is to know
   that Jesus is your friend!

Wave your arms, wave your arms
   and wave your arms again.
Oh how great it is to know
   that Jesus is your friend!

Turn around, turn around
   and turn around again.
Oh how great it is to know
   that Jesus is your friend!

Pray time

Our friend Jesus
Use the following prayer with the whole group; help children to join in with the response and with the simple actions. Say the prayer two or three times so that the children really grasp the words.

It's good to have a friend to talk to.
('Talk' hands.)
Thank you, Jesus, for being my friend!

It's good to have a friend who listens.
(Hand to ear.)
Thank you, Jesus, for being my friend!

It's good to have a friend to help me.
(All hold hands.)
Thank you, Jesus, for being my friend!

It's good to have a friend who loves me.
(Cross hands across chest in a hug.)
Thank you, Jesus, for being my friend!

Help me to be your friend too!

Extra time

- Make trees from cardboard tubes painted brown and fringed green crêpe paper foliage.

- Make drink and biscuit time into a special tea party by spreading a cloth on the table and having a special treat.

- Sing: 'Zacchaeus was a very little man', *JP* 300

'Whether you're one', *KS* 384
'Jesus, Jesus, here I am', *KS* 204
'Jesus is a friend of mine', (first verse only) *KS* 195
'Jesus love is very wonderful', *KS* 208
'Jesus is my friend', *KS* 197

Adults too

As you chat, comment that even though Zacchaeus was probably quite well hidden, sitting in his sycamore tree above the rest of the crowd, Jesus knew exactly where he was. He walked right up to the tree and called him by name. Jesus knows exactly where we are too. He knows our needs and our worries and he invites us by name to be his special friend. Zacchaeus was far from perfect, but Jesus still loved him. Jesus also loves us, 'warts and all', and his love can make a huge difference in our lives. Let others know, sensitively, that they can talk further about this to you or a church leader.

Top tip

If you don't have a special adult slot, you may find that the most natural time to share with the adults is during craft and making sessions when you can comment on the story while you work. Ask questions to help the children remember the story and add other details to give the parents or carers something extra to think about.

ACTIVITY PAGE:
The photocopiable activity page for this outline is on page 36

For your notes:

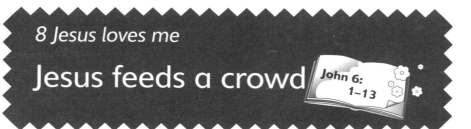

8 Jesus loves me
Jesus feeds a crowd
John 6: 1–13

each shape on a baking tray, leave to rise; then cook it. When cool, wrap each child's loaf in paper to take home.

If you do not have cooking facilities, make sandwiches using fish-flavoured spread and cut them into fish shapes with pastry cutters.

Teddy Bears' picnic
You will need: a picnic (either play or real), toy tea sets, teddies, blankets.

Help the children to spread out blankets, arrange teddies and set out the picnic. You could advertise this beforehand and encourage everyone to bring their own toy to the picnic. Let the children set everything out and enjoy serving and 'helping' the toys enjoy the picnic. They will enjoy imagining the food and drinks, but if you wish you could use play food or some real snacks.

Dough play
You will need: play dough.

Help the children to mould and make food for a picnic. These could be used for the Teddy Bears' picnic (above) or as props for the story, to be shared out (bread and fish shapes). If using salt or baking dough, cook the items before next time so you have hardened models for future play.

Sandwiches
You will need: sliced bread, rounded spreading knives, margarine, sandwich fillings, paper plates.

In a clean working area, and with clean hands, let the children spread slices of bread with margarine and a flavoured spread, then place another piece of bread on the top to make a sandwich. Have a range of fillings available so children can choose their favourite.

Nursery numbers
Sing or say nursery rhymes and songs which encourage counting, particularly twos and fives. Try: 'Five fat sausages', 'Five currant buns', 'Five little ducks went swimming', 'This old man', 'Once I caught a fish alive', 'Round and round the garden', 'Two little dicky birds'. Count sets of five and two objects. Count fingers, toes, eyes, ears, hands, feet, arms, legs.

Game time

5-7 mins

Let's go together
Play a game based on 'Going on a bear hunt'. All line up and follow a leader on a trek round the room. You will need some helpers mixed in among the children to keep them reasonably close together.

• Use the traditional bear or lion hunt wording as you go through long grass, over rivers and quickly home again.

• Go on a journey round your room or building and back again, describing what you see as you go, and making up actions and sound effects. Work out your route beforehand and think about which features to highlight.

• Pretend to be the people who followed Jesus one day to hear him speak, and who ate bread and fish with him, then went home again. Begin: 'We're going to follow Jesus, walk walk walk…'

Any of these variants can be played while walking on the spot; or even sitting and clapping to simulate walking along.

Making time

7-10 mins

Small loaves
You will need: packets of bread mix, bowls, baking trays, paper towels/napkins, cooking facilities, an extra adult helper.

Make sure the cooking area, the equipment and the children's hands are clean. Keep the children away from hot areas and have an adult responsible for using the oven.

Follow the instructions to make up the bread dough before the session or involve the children as much as possible in the process. Give each child a fist-sized piece and let them knead and shape it. Place

Story time

8-10 mins

One little lunch
You will need: five small bread rolls and two fish (canned or pretend!) wrapped in a cloth.

Here is a story about a boy who lived a long time ago. This boy kept hearing about a man called Jesus. Jesus sounded exciting! Jesus told interesting stories! Jesus made ill people better!

The boy decided to go and hear Jesus. His mum gave him a packed lunch, wrapped up in a little cloth. She gave him five little loaves of bread and two fish. 'Yummy, thanks!' said the boy, as he set off up the hill.

He followed the crowds of people and soon he saw Jesus standing in front of lots of people, speaking to them. The boy squeezed through the crowds and sat down. What wonderful stories he heard! Jesus was so interesting! The time flew by!

The boy's tummy started to rumble. Some other people nearby looked a bit hungry too. He heard Jesus' helpers talking. They looked worried. There were so many people, but there was no food. The boy opened his lunch. *(Open up your cloth bag.)* He had plenty of food for himself. Should he share it? He stood up and walked to Jesus' helpers. 'Excuse me,' he said, 'I have a little lunch here that I could share.'

The helpers said, 'Thank you.' They took the lunch to Jesus. It was enough food for a hungry boy. But there were more than five thousand people there that day. (That's too many to fit inside this room, even if they were all standing up: lots and lots of people!)

But Jesus didn't worry that there wasn't enough. He took the food and said a prayer. Then he started to share it out to the people nearby. The boy watched. Soon someone handed him some bread and fish. There was plenty for him, and he enjoyed eating it! Yum!

He watched lots of other people getting plenty too! There seemed to be more and more fish and bread. Much more than when he had carried it up the hill in the little cloth bag! The boy knew that Jesus had done something very special. Jesus had turned his little lunch into a wonderful meal for everyone!

Rhyme time

3-5 mins

Two fish and five little loaves
Say this rhyme through once, then add the finger actions. Repeat for everyone to join in.

This is the boy *(Hold up index finger.)*
Who had two fish,
    (Hold up two fingers on other hand.)
One, two fish,
And five little loaves.
    (Hold up five fingers.)
One, two, three, four, five little loaves.
He gave them all to Jesus.
    (Hold out hands.)

Here are the people,
    (Hold up and wiggle all fingers.)
Listening to Jesus. *(Hands by ears.)*
They had no food. *(Rub tummy.)*

Jesus thanked God for *(Raise hands.)*
The five loaves *(Five fingers.)*
And two little fish. *(Two fingers.)*
Then shared them with all the people.
    (Mime sharing.)

Also:

'Feeding the five thousand', *LACH* p55

Song time

3-5 mins

Lunch with Jesus
Pretend to be the people in the crowd as you sing, to the tune of 'There are hundreds of sparrows', KS 320. Sharing and eating real bread and fish fingers will add to the fun.

There were hundreds of people,
    thousands and thousands,
All listening to Jesus on the hill one day.

It was getting late and they all felt hungry,
But nobody wanted to go away.

There was one boy there
    who had brought a picnic,
Some fresh-made bread and a fish or two,
He gave his picnic dinner to Jesus,
And everyone wondered,
    'What will Jesus do?'

He shared the picnic with
    thousands and thousands,
The grown-ups and the children
    and the toddlers too,
A picnic for everyone –
    and more left over –
'Bread and fish for you and you
    and you and you.'

Pray time

3-4 mins

Wonderful Jesus
Declare how great Jesus is with this shout of praise. Say a few words and encourage everyone to repeat the phrase loudly and enthusiastically.

Jesus, how wonderful!
You fed the people on the hillside:
With just two fish and five little loaves
There was more than enough to eat!

Thank you, God
If you are eating together at any time today, copy the actions of Jesus before you eat. Hold up a piece of the food, look upwards and say thank you to God for the good food he gives us.
You can sing your thanks together by repeating the phrase 'Thank you, thank you, thank you God' six times to the tune of 'Twinkle twinkle little star'.

Extra time

•Read *The Lighthouse-keeper's Lunch*, by R and D Armitage, published by Scholastic, ISBN 0 59055 175 2.

•*Jesus feeds the people*, Little Fish books, published by SU, ISBN 0 85421 968 4.

•Make mobiles of bread and fish shapes.

•Sing 'God is good to me', '5000+ hungry folk', *KS* 2, 'Gives! Gives! Gives!' *KS* 67. Say 'I have sweets', *LSS* p88.

Adults too

Picnic time!
Organise a picnic outing after your meeting today to a nearby park, large garden or other safe area. You may be able to use a playground with toddler-sized equipment. If not, take some of your large play items (tricycles, tunnel, ride-on toys). Make sure everyone knows well in advance; bring some extra food so that new people or those who forget can still join in. If the weather isn't suitable, improvise indoors and pretend you're at the park on a lovely day! Socialising like this outside the normal group setting will help you all get to know each other better. (If everyone brought teddies for your play picnic, let them come to your real picnic too!)

Top tip

•*Share Out the Food with Jesus* by Stephanie Jeffs, published by SU, ISBN 1 85999 427 X, tells the story with bold bright illustrations. Smaller pictures show how to do actions to tell the story along with the storyteller.

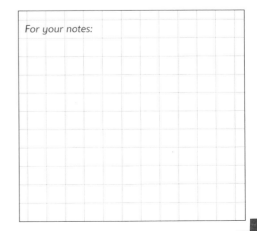

•Be safe! Make sure you have a record of any food allergies the children in your group suffer from. Check all ingredients carefully and do not allow the children to come into contact with their allergens during snack or cooking activities.

ACTIVITY PAGE:
The photocopiable activity page for this outline is on page 37

For your notes:

My name

Zacchaeus climbed a tree to see Jesus.

Can you colour in the pictures? Then cut out Zacchaeus and glue him onto the tree.

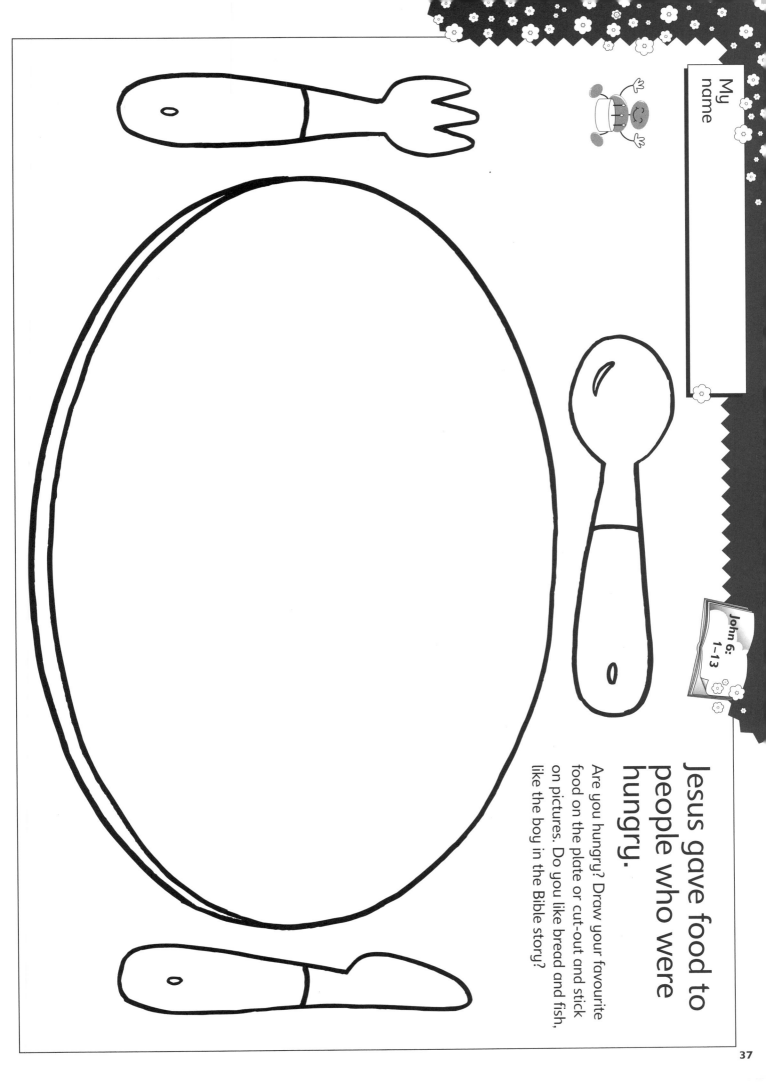

John 6: 1–13

Jesus gave food to people who were hungry.

Are you hungry? Draw your favourite food on the plate or cut-out and stick on pictures. Do you like bread and fish, like the boy in the Bible story?

9 Jesus loves me
Jesus stops the storm

Luke 8: 22–25

Play time

no limit

Water play

You will need: *large bowls or trays of water, plastic bowls, buckets, sieves, watering cans, plastic bottles, spoons, whisks, towels.*

Play outside, if the weather is suitable or in a 'wet play' area.

Be safe! Remove extra layers of clothing, roll sleeves up and provide aprons if available. Place the water containers on a table or stand as this is safer than water at ground level. Ensure that there is adult supervision at all times.

Allow and encourage the children to play freely.

Add new elements to the play with one or more of these options:

•washing-up liquid or baby bath and introduce whisks or sponges. (Use products suitable for sensitive skin.)

•ice cubes coloured with vegetable food colouring and spoons to stir the water. (Make sure that the children do not put the ice in their mouths.)

•plastic funnels, measuring jugs, bottles and cups.

Experiment with a variety of objects to see which will float and which will sink. Consider what is likely to happen with each object and then test it out. Try floating some toy boats – these don't always float well, so could be used as an example of sinking! What happens to your floating objects if you make waves in the water?

If you have a safe outside area, you could set up a paddling pool for the children to enjoy. Ensure plenty of supervision at all times with this activity and never leave it unattended.

Role play

Turn your 'home corner' into a boat: live on an ocean liner or a canal boat, or sail round the world in a yacht!

Game time

up to 15 mins

Magnetic fishing

You will need: *cardboard, collage scraps, PVA glue, metal paper clips, dowels or garden canes, string, small magnets, crêpe paper or fabric.*

Cut out fish shapes from card and decorate brightly with collage scraps. Clip one or two metal paper clips on the fish. Make fishing rods from the dowel, string and magnet. Make a river by spreading crumpled crêpe paper or fabric along the floor. Place the fish in the 'water' and help the children to use the rods to catch the fish. Have some plain fish to catch as well, as not all children will want to be involved in the whole process.

Making time

5-10 mins

Boats in bother

You will need: *cardboard egg boxes, card, stapler, paints, crayons, scissors, drinking or craft straws, sticky tape.*

Make model boats floating in the sea. Make the sea from the bottom of cardboard egg boxes, turned upside down and painted blue and green. Add a few white edges for realistic waves.

Cut two keel shapes from thin card, decorate with crayons or felt-tip pens, and staple the ends and bottom together.

Cut a rough square sail shape from a contrasting colour card. Make holes centre top and bottom, and push a long straw through for the mast. Make the sail tattered if you want it to look like a stormy scene. Push the end of the mast into the boat shape and secure with staples or tape.

Balance the boat between the lumps on the egg box sea.

Story time

10 mins

Jesus stops the storm

Act out the story, inviting the children to join you in your boat, made of chairs facing inwards. Throughout the story make sure that none of the children are getting anxious about it.

Would you like to come into my boat? *(Children sit on the chairs and in the 'well' in the middle. Brief an adult to be Jesus and settle down to sleep at the back but don't point this out until you need to wake him.)* We're going with Jesus across the sea. Let's all sit back and get comfortable. It's a lovely calm evening. Just rocking along gently in our boat.

Uh-oh. It's getting a bit dark. *(Dim room lights.)* Was that a spot of rain? Yes – it's started raining now. And it's getting a bit windy. Oooh! The waves are getting a bit rough. *(Sway.)*

And now there's a thunder storm starting. What a storm! Look out! There's water coming into the boat. Has anyone got a bucket? Quick – let's scoop out the water. *(Mime.)* The waves are getting ever so high! It's a terrible storm. I'm scared! What do you think we should do? The boat is going to sink! The boat is going to sink!

Jesus, the boat is going to sink! Jesus! Hey! Jesus is still asleep! WAKE UP JESUS! Come on everyone, shout to wake him up!

WAKE UP JESUS! One more time – **WAKE UP JESUS!**

(Jesus wakes – asks, 'What's the matter?')

Listen to the storm! It's raining, it's windy, the thunder and lightning are crashing and clashing! OUR BOAT IS GOING TO SINK!

(Jesus stands – holds out hand, points away from the boats and says 'Storm – be quiet! Waves – be still!' Pause.)

Listen – the storm has stopped. Look – the sea has calmed down. We're safe. Jesus has saved us. He told the storm to stop and it just stopped! Wow! Jesus is amazing. He's really, really special.

Here we are. We've reached the other side of the sea. Time to get out of the boat now. But don't forget who saved us, will you? Our friend Jesus. Thank you, Jesus!

Rhyme time

In the boat with Jesus
Act out the story to this rhyme, using puppets or people!

This is the boat that Jesus went in,
Sailing on the sea.
Jesus lay down and went to sleep
And the sea was as smooth as can be.

Then the wind began to blow.
His friends began to shout.
The water went splash into the boat.
They thought they'd be washed out.

This is the boat that Jesus went in,
Sailing on the sea.
Jesus told the wind to STOP!
And the sea was as smooth as can be.

Song time

The sails on the boat
Sing this song to 'The wheels on the bus', improvising simple actions.

The sails on the boat go up and down,
Up and down, up and down,
The sails on the boat go up and down
All night long.

The oars on the boat go splish
    and splash, …

The waves round the boat go crash,
    crash, crash, …

The people in the boat go wobble,
    wobble, wobble, …

Jesus in the boat goes zzzz, zzzz, zzzz, …

The people in the boat shout,
    'Wake up please,' …
'Wake up please.'

Jesus in the boat says, 'Waves be still,' …
'Waves be still.'

Jesus in the boat says, 'Wind be calm,' …
'Wind be calm.'

The wind and the waves go
    calm and still, …
Calm and still.

The people in the boat ask, 'Who is he?' …
'Who is he?'

Also:

'My God is so big', *KS* 255.

Pray time

Who is this man?
Use this responsive chant to affirm the power of Jesus for us today. Divide into two groups and practise saying alternate lines. A leader can answer the questions, while other leaders/adults support the children in asking the questions.

Children: Who is this man?
Leader: Even the winds and waves obey him.
Children: Who is this man?
Leader: He knows all our fears.
Children: Who is this man?
Leader: He is with us in the storm.
Children: Who is this man?
Leader: The Son of God! The Lord of all!
All: Jesus!

Extra time

•Play the traditional game 'The big ship sails on the ally-ally-o'. Sing 'The day I went to sea, sea, sea…' Sit on the floor and act out 'Row, row, row your boat'. Echo each other as you sing 'I hear thunder…'

•Make storm noises using rainsticks, long strips of cooking foil, plastic bottles, foil trays.

•Blow bubbles.

•Make boats from junk.

Adults too

During a local church mission, the team led a toddler afternoon of fun and games based on this story. While the adult carers were chatting after the story, a Muslim woman said, 'I know just how they felt. My little boy has cancer and the church here has been praying for him. Now I know Jesus is with us in all the storms of life.' The story of Jesus calming the storm often triggers a response from people who are going through tough times themselves. Without forcing confidences, be aware and alert to the needs of the adults in your group and ready to respond to them. It might be useful to have some helpful literature available, but the most valuable support you can give is yourself and your time.

Top tips

•Never leave water play areas unattended – a child can drown in a few centimetres of water.

•Set up an indoor water play in an area where the floor will not get slippery when wet.

•If playing outside on a sunny day, remember to use sunscreen and shaded areas.

•Have a few sets of spare clothes available!

ACTIVITY PAGE:
The photocopiable activity page for this outline is on page 42

For your notes:

Bartimaeus can see!

Mark 10: 46–52

Play time

 no limit

Group poster

You will need: a length of wallpaper, marker pen, scraps of coloured paper, PVA glue.

Among your free play activities include a collage table that the children can visit at some point during the Play time. In advance, write the name of your group in large outline letters on the plain side of the paper. Have ready some scraps of paper or fabric in a range of colours so that the children can decorate each letter in a different colour. Ask each adult to help two or three children to tackle a letter each and give them their collage pieces in a separate tub so that the colours don't get muddled. The finished poster should display a rainbow of colours. Explain that in the Bible story we are going to hear about a man who wasn't able to see all these wonderful colours.

Picture books

You will need: picture books.

In a corner pile up some cushions and set out colourful picture, pop up and lift the flap books. Ask an adult to sit and look at the books with the children. Talk about the pictures and colours, and invite the children to pick their favourite book and picture.

Sharp focus

You will need: spectacles, OHP and picture acetate.

Ask someone who wears spectacles to show them to the children and talk about how they help them to see clearly. If you have access to an OHP, show the children a picture completely out of focus and ask them to guess what it is, then focus the acetate while the children watch. Explain that spectacles help to bring the world around into focus for those who wear them.

Game time

 5 mins per game

Guessing game

Play a simple guessing game where the children have to guess who you are looking at. For example:

Do you know who I can see? No, who can you see? I can see someone with a ponytail and yellow dungarees; can you guess who it is?

I spy...

Adapt the traditional game so that you 'spy' items of a particular colour or shape, rather than by initial letter, eg 'I spy with my little eye something that is green'. If you play using letters, make sure you use the phonetic sound rather than the name of the letter.

Making time

 8 mins

Telescopes

You will need: cardboard kitchen roll tubes, circles of black paper, cling film, shiny or holographic gift wrap, PVA glue.

Take a long cardboard tube and cover one end with cling film. Tape the edges around the tube. Take a circle of black paper and cut a small peep hole in the centre. Fix this circle over the other end of the tube and tape the edges down. Finally, take a rectangle of shiny gift-wrap and glue it around the outside of your tube to make a shiny telescope.

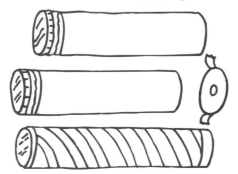

Story time

 5 mins

Bartimaeus can see!

You will need: an enlarged copy of the 'Bart' pictured below on A4 card, three extra faces, Blu-Tack.

Tell the story, using Blu-tack to fix a new expression on the face, as appropriate.

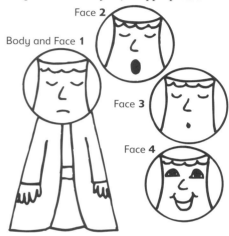

(Face 1) Bart was sad. He knew that everyone was happy and excited but he didn't know why. Poor Bart's eyes didn't work and he wasn't able to see. 'What's happening?' he called. 'Tell me what's happening!'

'Jesus is coming!' someone shouted to him. 'He's coming down the road now.'

Bart had heard all about Jesus. He'd heard how Jesus helped people who couldn't see or couldn't hear or couldn't walk. Bart wanted Jesus to help him. *(Add face 2.)* 'Jesus!' he called. 'Jesus! Please stop and help me!'

The people in the crowd turned round 'Shush! Be quiet!' they said. But Bart carried on shouting louder and louder!

Jesus stopped right where he was and said, 'Ask that man to come here.' Bart was amazed! *(Add face 3.)* Jesus was actually calling him.

'Come on!' said the crowd. 'Don't be afraid! He's calling you!' Bart threw off his coat, jumped up and stumbled over to Jesus as fast as his legs would take him.

'What do you want me to do for you?' said Jesus kindly. 'Oh Master!' replied Bart. 'I really want to be able to see!' And there and then Jesus made Bart's eyes better. *(Add face 4.)*

Bart looked around and he could see everything. He was so happy that he smiled and laughed and cheered. 'Thank you, thank you, thank you Jesus!' shouted Bart joyfully.

A little later Jesus and his friends carried on walking down the road, and Bart followed him too because he didn't want to let Jesus out of his sight.

Rhyme time

I see...

Invite ten children to stand in a line and act out the words of the following rhyme. Ask one child to sit down at the end of each couplet. If you have a large group, say the rhyme again with a different set of children.

I can see ten smiling children
    marching in a line,
One goes away and then there are nine.
I can see nine tall children
    standing up straight,
One goes away and then there are eight.
I can see eight happy children
    singing songs to heaven,
One goes away and then there are seven.
I can see seven happy children
    building with bricks,
One goes away and then there are six.
I can see six happy children
    awake and alive,
One goes away and then there are five.
I can see five happy children
    jumping on the floor,
One goes away and then there are four.
I can see three happy children
    waving at me,
One goes away and then
    there are three.
I can see three happy children
    with tidying up to do,
One goes away and then there are two.
I can see two happy children
    dancing, and having fun,
One goes away and then there is one.
I can see one happy child
    all on his/her own...
He/she went to join the others,
    so then there were none.

Song time

We can see

Sing the following simple words to the tune of 'Three Blind mice'.

We can see, we can see.
What can we see? What can we see?
God's beautiful world is everywhere,
The world he created
    with such great care,
So much beauty for us to share,
Since –
We can see... (*Repeat from the beginning.*)

Also:

'Here comes Bartimaeus', *LACH* p55
'Two little eyes', *KS* 345
'A sailor went to sea, sea, sea',
(traditional)

Pray time

Look around

Act out the following prayer by putting your hand to your eyes on 'Look around' and then scratching your head in puzzlement on 'What can I see?' Point towards the relevant things as they are named.

Look around... what can I see?
I can see you and I can see me!
I can see my friends, one, two, three!

Look around... what can I see?
I can see your head and
    I can see your toes!
I can see your eyes and
    I can see your nose!

Look around... what can I see?
I can see the window and
    I can see the door!
I can see the ceiling and I
    can see the floor!

Look around... what can I see?
I can see colours red, green and blue.
I can see books and lots of toys too!

Look around... there's so much to see!
So I say...
THANK YOU GOD
    for giving my eyes to me.

Extra time

•Show some slides through a handheld viewfinder, or use one of the toy viewfinders or slide shows.

•Blindfold a leader and ask them to guess who each child is just by the sound of their voice. Then, let some of the children have a go at wearing the blindfold.

Adults too

Bartimaeus wasn't too afraid or too embarrassed to call out to Jesus, and when the crowd tried to quieten him he simply called out again and louder. In the same way, Jesus wants us to turn to him when we are in need. Bartimaeus shows us that there's no need for long prayers with flowery words. He gets straight to the point. He used an arrow prayer: a short sharp prayer that hit the spot! You can pray arrow prayers anywhere at any time; they are instant prayers for special times of need. Bartimaeus also demonstrates that it's good to be persistent, he calls out to Jesus again and again. Paul gives the same advice in his letter to the Colossians (4:2), 'Be persistent in prayer...' Be prepared to listen to people's experiences of prayer, and don't be too quick to justify yourself or God if people have not received the response from God that they wanted.

Top tip

If you have any children in the group who suffer from visual impairment, make sure this material is used sensitively.

Consider how you can make your group more accessible and welcoming to children with any degree of visual impairment. 'Through the Roof' is an organisation which specialises in disability ministry: log on to www.throughtheroof.org for more information.

ACTIVITY PAGE:
The photocopiable activity page for this outline is on page 43

My name

Jesus had the power to make the storm stop!

Look at the pictures and tell the story to a friend.

My name

Mark 10: 46–52

Thank you, God, for eyes to see.

Can you see these things in the big picture? Look and see. When you find them, colour in the little picture. Then colour the whole page.

| flower | sun | tree | cat | toys | dog | bird | squirrel |

... I make music

2 Chronicles 20

Play time

Jigsaws

Make simple jigsaws for the children to complete by mounting pictures of instruments on card and cutting up.

Band together

You will need: musical instruments, pots, pans, wooden spoons, tape recorder and tapes, toy microphone.

Avoid making the whole of your Play time noisy by putting out equipment for a limited time only.

•Have some old pots and pans and wooden spoons for the children to play with. Encourage them to form a band.

•Place a box of instruments alongside a cassette recorder and some nursery rhyme tapes. Join with them and put a blank tape in the recorder to tape their singing and playing. Play it back to them.

•Many bands, choirs and orchestras have a uniform. Find a number of coloured tabards, sashes, bow ties, or armbands for the children to wear. March around together with drums, tambourines and shakers.

•Play marching games around the room using songs such as 'Grand Old Duke of York' and 'We are marching.' (JU p34,)

•Borrow some real instruments for the children to look at and investigate.

•Pass a toy microphone around the circle allowing each child to choose a favourite song to sing. Suggest that they sing it either on their own or with the group.

Doh ray me

Put out a selection of rhyme and songbooks, including hymn and music books. If you are musical, demonstrate how the notes on the page tell you what note to play or sing. If possible, have some books that incorporate a mini-keyboard with colour-coded notes and keys. Encourage the children to play along.

Game time

Musical bumps

Play a simplified version of musical bumps. When the music stops, everyone should clap those who remember to sit down. Try again until everyone remembers to sit down. Then try getting them to sit on a mat when the music stops.

Musical friends

Play a few bars of the theme tunes and songs to popular children's television programmes. Have pictures of the characters associated with each tune. Ask the children to listen carefully and choose which character goes with which tune. They may like to join in singing the songs once they have guessed.

Which one?

Sit in a circle and place a selection of different instruments in the middle. Have a duplicate set hidden in a box. Play one instrument at a time and invite the children to guess which instrument you are playing.

Making time

 5-10 mins

Make and shake

You will need: transparent plastic bottles or film containers, coloured pasta shapes or rice, sticky tape, streamers made from crêpe paper.

Part fill a plastic bottle with pasta shapes. Secure the top with sticky tape and attach streamers. Or, fill plastic film containers with rice; secure the lid well.

Ring-a-ding

You will need: polystyrene cups or sections of an egg box, chenille wires, bells, adhesive shapes, glitter, felt-tip pens.

Pierce two holes in the base of either a polystyrene cup or a section of an egg box. Thread a chenille wire through the holes and secure a bell inside the bell holder. Twist the wire to make a handle. Decorate with adhesive shapes, glitter and felt-tip pens.

Also:

Craft books *Here's One I Made Earlier* (ISBN 0 86201 981 8) and *Here's Another One I Made Earlier*, (ISBN 1 85999 338 9) published by SU, have further suggestions for making musical instruments.

Story time

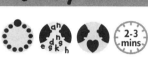 2-3 mins

Sing with the king!

You will need: 5 faces – a king, man, woman, child and baby made from paper plates fastened on to sticks so that you can pick them up quickly and easily.

Hold up the faces as they appear in the story.

There was once a king with a BIG problem. An army was coming to attack his people. 'I don't know what to do!' he said. 'We must ask God.'

And so he called all the people to the temple. All the men came. All the women came. All the children came. And all the babies came too – their mums and dads carried them.

Everyone came to the temple. Everyone prayed to God. Everyone asked God, 'What can we do?' As they were praying, God spoke. 'Don't be afraid,' God said. 'This is my battle, not yours. You will meet the army, but you will not have to fight. I will be with you.'

'Wow!' said the king. 'God has spoken to us. God has told us what to do. Let's say thank you to God! Let's sing praises to God! Let's make joyful music to God!' And so they did. The men made joyful music.

The women made joyful music. The children made joyful music. And the babies made joyful music – very loudly!

The next day the people did as God said. They marched off to meet the army with everyone making joyful music. When they arrived, guess what they saw? Nothing! No fighting. No screaming. No shouting. The battle was over – the people of the army, which was coming to attack them, had fought against each other instead!

'Hooray!' said the king.

'Hooray!' said the men.

'Hooray!' said women.

'Hooray!' said the children.

'Hooray!' said the babies - in a baby kind of way!

Then the king said, 'God has won the battle. Let everyone thank and praise God.' So they all went back to the temple to praise God and make joyful music.

Shall we make music like the king and his people?

Play some joyful music, give out instruments and march around your room to the sound of the music.

Rhyme time

  2-3 mins

Making joyful music

Encourage the children to make sad, bad and glad faces at the appropriate point. Give out instruments for use only during the refrain line, 'When the people made joyful music'. You could also use the visual aids from the story.

The king was very sad,
The army was very bad,
But God was very glad,
When the people made joyful music.

Continue with:
The men were very sad…
The women were very sad….
The children were very sad…
The babies were very sad….

End with:
Sometimes we feel very sad,
When things seem really bad,
But God helps us to be glad,
When we make joyful music.

Song time

   4-5 mins

Let's praise!
Make joyful music to these two songs. Adapt the words to suit the musical instruments you have available. Sing to 'Do you know the muffin man?'

Let's praise God with instruments,
    with instruments, with instruments,
Let's praise God with instruments,
    he loves to hear us play.

Let's praise God shh quietly, shh quietly,
    shh quietly…

Let's praise God loudly, loudly, loudly…

Sing to 'Wind the bobbin up'.

Play your instruments,
Play your instruments,
Shake, shake, (or ring, or bang, or click)
We're praising God!
    Play your instruments,
    Play your instruments,
    Shake, shake, we're praising God!
Play them high, and play them low,
    Play them fast , and play them slow,
Play with the beat now – one, two, three,
Then put them down very quietly!

Pray time

   1 min

Musical prayers
A prayer rhyme to be read by a leader. Encourage the children to join in the refrain line: 'We thank you heavenly father'.

For drums to beat and tunes so sweet,
We thank you heavenly father.

For bells to ring and songs to sing,
We thank you heavenly father.

For clappers to clap and streamers to flap,
We thank you heavenly father.

That we can play joyful music to say:
Thank you heavenly father.

Using instruments can develop this prayer. Practise first, so that children know when they are to play (and stop!). Lead the prayer strongly as children will be concentrating on their playing and need extra help to listen to the words as well.

Extra time

•Read *Music Makers: Teddy Horsley*, published by CEC, ISBN 1 85175 077 0.

•If you have an organ or piano in church, try to arrange for someone to come in to play it to the children.

•Have a selection of children's instruments available for borrowing. Parents and carers may be reluctant to buy these and they may appreciate the opportunity to borrow for a short period of time!

Adults too

We all face problems from time to time where we cry out 'I don't know what to do!' Jehoshaphat directed his cry to God in prayer. There will almost certainly be adults in or linked to your group who are asking and looking for direction of some kind in their lives. Find an appropriate way of making prayer accessible to them. It may be simply giving them a card, starting a prayer book, board or box in which they can place any requests (assure them that God knows the details and they don't need to record this unless they particularly want to), or a safe place where a candle can be lit. God loves to hear our cry for help but even more; he loves to answer prayer – even if it isn't quite what we're expecting!

Top tip

When using musical instruments be sure to:

•Store them separately from the rest of the toys;

•Check them regularly for damage (especially on home-made ones);

•Wipe then clean after each session;

•Avoid instruments that go into the mouth, eg recorder, mouth organ;

•Give them out for specific songs and collect them in afterwards.

ACTIVITY PAGE:
The photocopiable activity page for this outline is on page 48

12 God loves it when...

... I sing

Psalm 19

Play time

Pop stars

You will need: toy microphones (or home-made ones from a tube of card with a plastic ball fixed to one end), tape recorder, blank tape.

Set up the equipment and encourage the children to pretend they are pop stars and record themselves singing.

Sleepy time

You will need: dolls, prams, cots, bedding, baths, tape or CD player and gentle music.

Set up a home corner with dolls, prams, cots, bedding and baths. Play gentle music in the background like lullabies, pan pipe or classical music. Listen out for any spontaneous singing that might accompany the children's playing.

Nursery songs

You will need: jigsaws, picture books, and colouring books based on nursery rhymes and songs.

Consider making rhyme cards by cutting out the pages of these books and mounting them onto card. Lamination will make them even more durable. Encourage the children to identify the rhyme or song and sing it.

Sing and play

You will need: a toy farmyard with model animals and machinery.

Play a recording of 'Old Macdonald had a Farm' in the background and encourage the children to listen to the words of the song as they play.

Nursery craft

Set up a craft table to make objects from nursery rhymes, eg spiders to use with 'Incy Wincy Spider', five duck prints on a paper plate for 'Five little ducks went swimming'. Choose the children's favourite songs.

Noisy time!

You will need: a tape or CD player, instruments, lively party or praise music.

Give out instruments and create plenty of space for the children to jump around and dance while they are playing their instruments. This can be useful to burn off energy before settling down to a circle or story time. Be sensitive to those who don't want to join in.

Game time

What shall we sing?

Walk round in a circle singing to the tune 'Here we go Looby Lou':

What shall we sing today?
What shall we sing today?
What shall we sing today?
Who will choose us a song?

Invite one child at a time to select a song of their choice. They may like to stand in the circle and sing it to the rest of the children, but don't put them under pressure to do so.

Make up a song box containing different objects that might prompt the children to think of a song, eg bus ('Wheels on the bus'), sheep ('Baa, baa, black sheep'), star ('Twinkle, twinkle little star'), red heart ('Jesus' love is very wonderful'). Bring out each item individually and ask the children what to sing. Include TV characters, eg Bob the Builder, Postman Pat.

Making time

My favourite songs

You will need: A3 sugar paper, copies of the words to some favourite songs printed in a large font, glue, crayons.

Make a book of favourite songs for each child to take home. Fold an A3 piece of sugar paper into quarters, staple or stitch the centre and cut across the top fold to make an eight-page book. Print in large font size the words of some of the children's favourite songs. Include a mixture of nursery rhymes and Christian songs. (You may use words of songs and rhymes from *Tiddlywinks* Big Books for this activity.) Make sure there are more songs than pages so that the children will have to decide which are their favourites. Encourage them to stick their songs into their books and illustrate them.

Story time

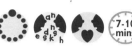

David sings

You will need: a simple tunic, a shepherd's headdress, toy sheep and lion or bear, a homemade harp, crown.

Dress a child up as David, adding each of these items at the asterisked stage of the story. Tell the children that you are going to tell them about someone who loved to sing – everywhere and anywhere.

David * was a special friend of God. He loved to sing. When he was small, he sang at home with his mum and dad. He sang with his brothers, all seven of them. He sang in the kitchen, outside, in his bed, on long journeys and when he went to worship God. Everywhere David went he learned to sing songs.

David became a shepherd boy* looking after sheep* in the fields. Sometimes he got scared at night and worried that the bears* and lions* would come to take his sheep. So he sang a song to God. God helped him to be brave.

David made up his own songs. He played them on his harp.* He sang about the stars, and the moon, the mountains and the trees. He sang all about God's love, how great and wonderful he is.

Everyone heard about David's beautiful songs. Everyone loved his singing – even the king!

'Come and sing your happy songs to me,' said the king. 'Then I will feel happy too.'

And so David took his harp and went to live in the king's palace. David sang his happy songs whenever the king asked. Everyone loved David and his songs. Everyone wanted David to be king*.

So, he became king. When he was king, he sometimes got very lonely. He felt sad and frightened when he had to fight in battles. He worried about the important decisions he had to make. What do you think David did? Yes – he sang more songs.

David sang when he was small and he sang when he was tall. He could sing when he was glad. And he could sing when he was sad. Wherever he was, however he felt, he knew that God was with him when he sang.

Ask the children what songs they might sing when they are happy, sad, frightened or lonely.

Rhyme time

Sing!
Make up some simple actions to go with this rhyme.

Sing when you're tiny,
Sing when you're small,
Sing when you're growing fast,
Sing when you're tall.

Sing when you're feeling down,
Sing when you're sad,
Sing when you're all alone,
And you will soon be glad.

Sing about the skies so high,
Sing about the moon,
Sing about the twinkling stars,
Sing a happy tune.

Sing about the love of God,
Sing about his care,
Sing about how he made you,
And children everywhere.

Song time

Songs for singing
Sing to the tune of 'London bridge is falling down'.

David sang when he was small, he was small, he was small,
David sang when he was small,
He sang to God.

David sang when he was tall, he was tall, he was tall,...

David sang when he was scared, he was scared, he was scared,...

David sang when he was glad, he was glad, he was glad,...

We can sing when we are.... *(Choose any of the above or make up your own.)*
We sing to God.

Sing to the tune of 'Row, row, row your boat.'

Sing, sing, sing your songs,
Sing them all day long,
Jesus loves it when we sing,
All our lovely songs.

Pray time

We are praying
Sing this gentle quiet prayer song to God to the tune of 'Kumbaya'.

We are praying Lord, with a song,
We are praying Lord, with a song,
We are praying Lord, with a song,
You hear us all day long.

We say thank you Lord, with a song,...
And you hear us all day long.

We say sorry Lord, with a song,...
And you hear us all day long.

Extra time

•Read *The Song: Teddy Horsley*, published by CEC, ISBN 1851751440.

•Invite a singer/musician to visit your group to sing to and with the children.

•Have background music playing throughout your session today.

•Listen to different kinds of singers, eg, popular, jazz, classical, folk, and music from different cultures (African, Asian, Scottish, Spanish).

•Learn a song to sing as a grace for your refreshment time, like 'Thank you for the world so sweet.'

Adults too

David's songs are recorded for us in the Psalms. They express a wide spectrum of emotions from ecstasy, elation, thanksgiving and praise to extreme anger, sorrow, doubt, bitterness and guilt. He loves God, hides from God, challenges and questions God through the words of the psalms. There is hardly a human emotion known to humankind that David doesn't experience or express. They were the pop songs of the Jewish people!

Take a look at some of the lyrics of modern day pop songs that parents and carers may be familiar with. Compare the questions presented and emotions experienced with some of the psalms. Invite adults to choose a song they like and say why. What do they play (or sing) when they are happy, sad, lonely, etc? Use this as a springboard for discussion about hopes, fears, dreams and questions of faith. Remind everyone that God can deal with our doubts, questions and anger.

Top tip

•Unaccompanied singing is beneficial for young children; instruments can be a distraction at times.

•Sit at a child's level in a circle where everyone can see you.

•Young children have a limited vocal range: on average only six pitches from D above middle C to B (a sixth above). Keep all songs within that range. Try using a recorder or chime bars (C or D) to give a starting note.

ACTIVITY PAGE:
The photocopiable activity page for this outline is on page 49

My
name

God loves it when I make music.

The king led the people, singing and playing trumpets and harps.
How many trumpets can you count?
How many harps can you count?

2 Chronicles 20

God loves it when I sing.

Look at the pictures. Can you sing a song about what you see?

What song do you like singing best? Draw a picture of it here. Then sing that song to God!

Psalm 19

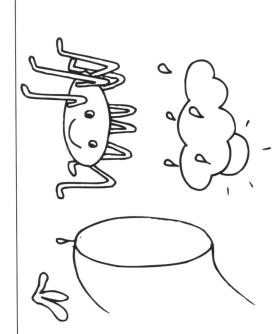

13 God loves it when...

... I dance

Exodus 15: 19–21

Also:

Craft books *Here's One I Made Earlier* (ISBN 0 86201 981 8) and *Here's Another One I Made Earlier*, (ISBN 1 85999 338 9) published by SU, have further suggestions for making musical instruments.

Play time

 no limit

Jumping joints

You will need: simple skeleton bodies with knee, hip, elbow, shoulder, waist and neck joints hinged with split pins; colouring and collage materials.

Help the children to make skeletons or make them beforehand. Let them colour or collage their skeletons. Help the children to explore the different parts of the skeleton and relate that to their own bodies. Develop a simple game where each child in turn puts their own 'skeleton' (their bodies) into a position that everyone else has to try to copy (with their own bodies).

Let's dance!

You will need: a variety of dance costumes, eg leotard, tutu, ballet shoes, tap shoes, silky scarves and ribbons, wrist bells, streamers.

Dress up in the costumes and dance to a variety of background music, ranging from pop/party music to classical ballet and Morris dancing jigs. Dance to the theme tune from *The Snowman*, 'Walking in the Air' or Saen Sans' 'Carnival of the Animals'. Try some electronic music and dance like machines or robots. Dance together in circles, choosing familiar dancing songs such as 'Ring-a-roses', 'Hokey cokey' and 'The farmer's in his den'. Make up simple dance movements and words for a circle dance using other tunes such as 'The bear went over the mountain' ('We dance around in a circle... we dance just like a pop star/ballerina/elephant/old man'). Encourage the children to suggest ways in which you can dance together – and to interpret that character in their own ways.

Streamers and jingles

You will need: crêpe paper, sticky tape, thick chenille wires, bells, Velcro.

Make streamers and jingles that the children can wear as they dance. Tape strips of brightly coloured crêpe paper to a thick chenille wire; twist these to make bracelets, hairclips or headbands. Or sew bells on to strips of Velcro, long enough to fasten round wrists, ankles or below the knee, like traditional English Morris dancers.

Game time

 5-10 mins

Move with the music

Play a simplified version of musical statues: dance to the music until it stops – then everyone has to try to stand still.

Play a simplified version of 'Simon says' giving dance-related instructions eg, 'Simon says dance like a butterfly... a ballet dancer... a rabbit... an elephant...'

Sing plenty of action rhyme songs that make full use of movement of the body, eg 'Heads, shoulders, knees and toes', 'I'm a dingle dangle scarecrow', 'The grand old Duke of York', 'Ring a ring o'roses', 'Hokey cokey'.

Making time

 5 mins

Tambourines

You will need: paper plates, rice, staplers, sticky tape, hole punch, strips of card, coloured crêpe paper or ribbons, sticky shapes or felt-tip pens, chenille wires, bells (The last two are optional).

Place a spoonful of rice on a plate. Put a second plate, upside down, on top of it and staple around the inside of the rims so that no rice can escape. Tape over the sharp ends of the staples with sticky tape. Cut out strips of card which can be taped to the tambourine as handles. Punch holes through the outside of the rims and attach streamers or chenille wires with bells threaded on. Decorate the plates with sticky shapes or draw on patterns with felt-tip pen.

Story time

 2 mins

Miriam dances

You will need: a big mouth puppet made from an old sock to be Miriam – allow her to tell her own story to the children.

Practise co-ordinating the mouth with your words beforehand and use the head movement to express feelings and emotions.

Hello – my name is Miriam, and I've come to tell you my story.

My family are friends of God. When I was little I learned all about God and his people, just like you. I heard wonderful stories, sang lovely songs and went to the temple with my family. My brothers, Moses and Aaron, became leaders of God's people. I helped them and sometimes God gave me special messages for them.

One day something amazing happened. All God's people lived in Egypt, but they were sad and frightened. The king didn't like us and he was very cruel to us. We tried to escape but his army chased us all the way to the sea. Moses said, 'Don't worry, God will take care of us'. And he was right!

God sent a strong wind to push back the sea so that we could walk across to the other side. When the army tried to follow, God sent the water pouring back. We were safe! We were free! We were happy again! Everyone was amazed. I started to sing. I sang and sang and sang. And then I started to dance. All the women followed me. We danced and sang and danced and sang all night long. And we played our tambourines. Everyone was so happy that God had saved his people. It was a very special night.

How to make a Miriam puppet

1 Cut a triangle from the toe end of an adult-size sock.

2 Cut 8–10 cm circles of stiff card and flesh-coloured felt.

Cut card in two and tape it back together again. This is the mouthpiece.

3 Push the mouth into the sock end and stick the cut edges around the edge of the card mouthpiece. (A glue gun is ideal.)

4 Cover the card with felt, covering the rough glued edges.

5 Stuff the sock with cotton wool to give a raised head shape and decorate with felt eyes, nose, tongue and wool hair.

Rhyme time

 2-3 mins

Dance like this...

This is the way the babies dance,
Wriggly wriggle, wriggly wriggle,
This is the way the babies dance,
Wriggly, wriggle, wriggle.

This is the way the little girls dance,
On tippety toes, tippety toes…

This is the way the little boys dance,
Like jumping beans, jumping beans…

This is the way the teenagers dance,
Shakety shake, shakety shake…

Try: mummies, daddies, grandmas, giraffes, little mice… Ask the children to suggest how!

Song time

 3-4 mins

Dance with Miriam

Sing and dance to 'She'll be coming round the mountain'.

We can sing and dance and
    play like Miriam,
We can sing and dance and
    play like Miriam,
We can sing and dance and play,
To praise God here today,
We can sing and dance and
    play like Miriam.

Use the chorus-tune of 'Lord of the dance'. Move around the room when singing this song with different children leading the dance in their own way.

Fo-llow follow follow me,
I am the leader of the dance you see,
And I'll lead you all wherever you may be,
And I'll lead you all in a dance with me.

Pray time

 3-5 mins

Be still
***You will need:** a bottle of bubble mixture.*

Explain to the children that bubbles can help us to focus on our prayers. Each time we blow a bubble we can think about sending a prayer to God. When it bursts it reminds us that God hears our prayers and we can all say, 'Amen'.

Offer one-line thank you prayers before blowing each bubble, eg, 'Thank you God for ears to hear lovely music… voices to sing… instruments to play… legs to dance…'

Encourage the children to watch the bubble quietly and join together to say, 'Amen' when it bursts. Invite the children to suggest their own one-line thank you prayers.

Extra time

•Tell the story of when David danced from 2 Samuel 6:14 in your own words.

•Use one of the 'Sticky Fingers' series of tapes for a music and movement session, available from Sticky Music, PO Box 176, Glasgow, G4 9ER.

•'Let's all clap hands', *LACH* p13
'Move it!' *LACH* p88
'Jump and sing', *LACH* p42
'Dance and sing', *LSS* p17
'Let's sing and shout', *LSS* p19

Adults too

Miriam was an interesting character and many won't connect her with the young girl who watched over the baby Moses in the basket. Years later she went on to play a significant role in supporting Moses and Aaron her brothers in their leadership of God's people. She was recognised as a prophetess and became one of the early women leaders in Israel but is first featured in the Bible as a sister and dancer!

Many of us play hugely important roles in the background of other people's lives as someone's sister, father, mother, wife, husband, partner or carer. Many selflessly put on hold their own careers, interests and hobbies but feel devalued and worthless as our society places low value on their roles. Spend some time affirming the carers and parents in your group and the life-changing and life-enhancing work they do. Remind them of Ecclesiastes 3:1 'there is a time for everything under heaven.'

Top tip

Movement and dance is a wonderful way to encourage young children to exercise but they need safe space in which to do it. Think carefully about the layout of your room for this session. Consider putting out less equipment. If your room is small, think of creative ways of using other space in the building, eg wide corridors, a carpeted area of your church, or a grassy area outdoors. Remove any dangerous obstacles and consider making a barrier of chairs to keep the children contained in one area when they are dancing.

ACTIVITY PAGE:
The photocopiable activity page for this outline is on page 54

For your notes:

... I look at books

2 Kings 22, 23

Play time

no limit

Lost treasure
You will need: A3 size gold card with 'God's Special Book' written on the front and cut into six pieces to make a jigsaw.

Either bury the jigsaw pieces in a sandpit or hide them around the room for children to find. When all the pieces have been gathered, work together to assemble the puzzle. (This could also be used as an introduction to your Story time.)

Book corner
You will need: books, comfortable seats or cushions.

Create a special area for looking at books. Try to provide comfortable seating, a carpet area or cushions and take time to display a variety of different kinds and sizes of books for children to handle and look at. Include picture books, recipe books, wordbooks, maps, prayer books and Bibles, as well as favourite storybooks. You might also like to include some story tapes.

Tidy-up time
•If you have a home corner, ensure you have dusters, buckets, brooms and brushes out today. Encourage a cleaning and sorting day.

•Sort through your toy boxes to see if there is anything that needs to be re-sorted, cleaned or repaired. Involve the children in washing dolls; wiping building blocks and making sure all the jigsaw pieces are present. Emphasise the importance of looking for things that have been lost and keeping them in good order.

•Take the opportunity to clear out your bookshelves. Give the children dusters, pans and brushes, and perhaps even water and cloths to clean the shelves. Sort all the different books and put them back tidily on the shelves or bookstand. Repair any damaged books too. Let the children help you with these jobs.

Game time

5 mins

I need a book
Play this game by singing this rhyme to the tune of 'Three Blind Mice'. Place a variety of books in the middle of the circle and invite the children to find the right book.

I need a book, I need a book,
Which will it be, which will it be?
I need a book to help me cook,
I need a book to help me cook,
I need a book to help me cook,
Please find a book for me!

Additional verses:

I need a book to sing a song (music book).

I need a book to say my prayers (prayer book).

I need a book to show me the way (map).

I need a book to mend a chair (DIY).

I need a book to help me garden (gardening book).

I need a book to learn about God (Bible).

Making time

4-5 mins

Bookmarks
You will need: brightly coloured card, glue sticks, hole punch, sticky shapes,

crayons and felt-tip pens, coloured wool or thick silky thread, templates.

Make a special bookmark to go into the children's favourite book. Use good quality card and materials for this, as you want them to treasure and keep it. If possible, arrange for the bookmarks to be laminated to give extra durability. Consider some of the designs suggested or use letter templates for each child's name.

Scrapbooks
You will need: sugar paper, glue, scissors, pictures.

Children love making their own books: set out the equipment and help them to make a book. Then let them do their own thing to fill it.

Story time

5-7 mins

God's special book
You will need: three stick puppets of the same king with a sad face, a talking face and a happy face; toy tools – a saw, hammer and chisel; a large old Bible sprinkled with talcum powder to look like dust.

Use the visual aids at the appropriate asterisked stage of the story.

Josiah was a good king*. He loved God and took care of God's house, the temple. He paid carpenters*, builders* and masons* to do lots of repair jobs on the temple. They were busy, busy, busy all day long.

One day, when everyone was working hard in the temple, the priest found a very old book* underneath all the builders' rubble. It was dusty* and nobody had opened it for a very long time.

'What is this?' He said, 'I must show the king.'

King Josiah read the book. *

'STOP!' Josiah said to the people.

'LISTEN!' Josiah said to the people. 'This is no ordinary book. It is the Book of God's Law. It shows us how God wants us to live.'

King Josiah was sad. * King Josiah was very, very sad. King Josiah knew that God's people had not been living God's way.

'Come to the temple,' he said. 'Listen to

God's law. Get rid of everything that makes God sad. From now on, promise to live God's ways!'

And the people did just that. They came. They listened. And they promised to live God's way - all because they found God's special book.

Story extra

Read the story of Moses receiving God's special rules for living on Mount Sinai from a children's Bible. Explain that these rules were in the book that was found when the men were mending the temple.

Rhyme time

What's in the Bible?

Find some answers to the question with this rhyme. You could make up a melody to sing along with too.

What's in the Bible?
Lots of things, lots of things.
Tales of people long ago,
That's what's in the Bible.

What's in the Bible?
Lots of things, lots of things.
Rules to help us live each day,
That's what's in the Bible.

What's in the Bible?
Lots of things, lots of things.
Messages from God to us,
That's what's in the Bible.

What's in the Bible?
Lots of things, lots of things.
Songs that people sing to God,
That's what's in the Bible.

What's in the Bible?
Lots of things, lots of things.
Stories of Jesus to enjoy,
That's what's in the Bible.

What's in the Bible?
Lots of things, lots of things.
Letters Paul wrote to his friends,
That's what's in the Bible.

Song time

God's word

Explain that the Bible is full of God's written-down words to us. Then sing to the tune of 'The bear went over the mountain'.

God's word is very special,
  God's word is very special,
God's word is very special,
  it shows us how to live.

We read about God's people,
  we read about God's people,
We read about God's people,
  they show us how to live.

We read about Jesus, we read about Jesus,
We read about Jesus,
  he shows us how to live.

God's special book

Make the same point with these words to 'Twinkle, twinkle little star.'

The Bible is God's special book,
The Bible is God's special book,
The Bible tells me God loves me,
And shows me how I ought to be,
The Bible is God's special book,
The Bible is God's special book.

Pray time

Best books

Place a selection of children's Bible storybooks in the centre of a circle. Invite each child to choose their favourite one and bring it to a special table where it can be displayed. As each one does this, stop and pray together saying:

'Thank you God for the story of … in the Bible.'

Show a children's prayer book to the children, open it and read one or two short prayers from it, choosing topics which will appeal to your particular group.

End your prayer time by singing together the first verse of the song 'God's word' (Song time above).

Extra time

•Sing 'God loves you so much', *KS* 81.

•Contact your local Christian bookshop to arrange for a sale or return bookstall of appropriate children's Bibles and storybooks. Many parents and adults are keen to buy books of this kind, but do not have access to the specialist bookshops.

•*Here's One I made Earlier*, published by SU, ISBN 0 86201 981 8, has pages of ideas for how to make your own books. Why not try some out!

•Set the construction toys out and repair the temple for Josiah!

Adults too

Living life according to God's rules, eg the Ten Commandments, is a challenging topic for discussion with adults in the 21st century! Evangelist, J John has produced a series of videos called *Take 10* based on the commandments. His preaching on this theme has produced some incredible responses. Consider making these available for loan or arranging a series of adult sessions to watch and discuss them together. Contact The Philo Trust, 141 High Street, Rickmansworth, Herts, WD3 1AR for further information.

Take the opportunity to encourage personal Bible reading for the young and older. *Tiddlywinks: My Little Books* (six titles) are designed for children and their carers to use together as they take their first steps into Bible reading. See page 89 for details. And Scripture Union produces a wide range of adult Bible notes for personal and group use too. Check out: www.scriptureunion.org.uk/publishing

Top tip

Whenever you tell a Bible story make sure that both children and adults know that it is from the Bible. Always have an appropriate children's Bible visible and refer to it before or after the story. Good Bibles for this age group include *The Beginners Bible*, published by Zondervan, ISBN 0 31092 610 6 and the *Lion First Bible,* published by Lion, ISBN 0 74593 210 X. Children will be interested in seeing your personal Bible too: you can show them the same story and demonstrate book-handling skills (how you find the right place, turning pages carefully, etc).

ACTIVITY PAGE:
The photocopiable activity page for this outline is on page 55

God loves it when I dance.

Join Miriam and the women dancing. Draw yourself dancing at the end of the line. What musical instrument will you play?

Exodus 15: 19–21

My name

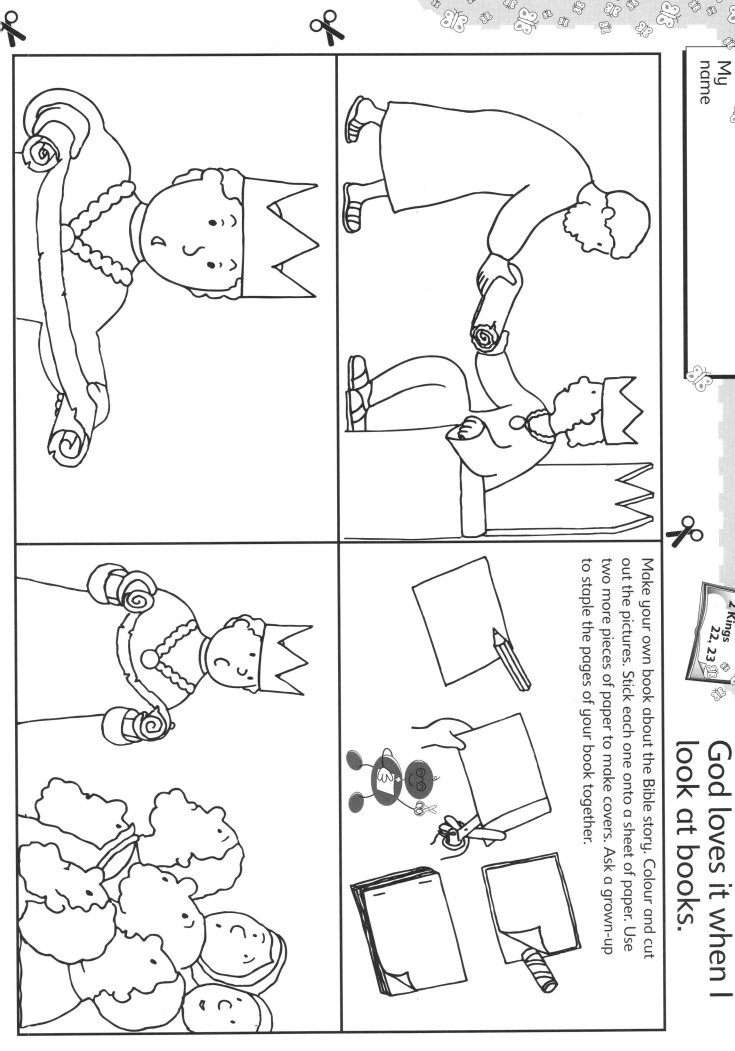

My name

2 Kings 22, 23

God loves it when I look at books.

Make your own book about the Bible story. Colour and cut out the pictures. Stick each one onto a sheet of paper. Use two more pieces of paper to make covers. Ask a grown-up to staple the pages of your book together.

15 God loves it when...

... I'm 'me'!

Psalm 139

2-3 mins

Who made me?

You will need: *a 'talking' puppet to represent a child. Make a hand puppet from an old sock or mitten; or see page 50/51 for instructions.*

This dialogue is based on the fact that children are always asking questions, with answers based on Psalm 139.

Jean?

Yes Mickey?

Who made me, Jean?

God made you Mickey, just like he made all the children here today.

If God made them and God made me why don't we look the same?

That's because God made you special Mickey. He made you 'you' and he made each of the children different too.

How did he make them different?

Well, he made some small, and others tall, gave some brown eyes, some green eyes... *(describe some of the children in your group).*

Are we all different Jean? Everyone in the whole wide world?

Yes Mickey – everyone in the whole wide world is different – just as God made him or her.

Wow – God's very clever isn't he Jean?

He certainly is Mickey. You know, not only did he make us different, he knew exactly what we would look like before we were born.

How could he know that?

Because God could see us inside our mummies' tummies.

How?

God can see everything Mickey. He knows when you sit down and when you get up. He knows when you are asleep and when you are playing. Whatever you are doing and wherever you are, God knows and sees you.

Can he see me when I play with my toys?

Yes.

Can he see me when I'm eating tea?

Play time

no limit

Good play

Play is central to this session because when children play they are being themselves. Try hard to provide a variety of different play opportunities (physical, creative, constructive, etc) so that they can choose what they do. What they choose will reflect their individual preferences and characters and they will be 'being' themselves. Structure your Play time so that a selection of activities is put out at different times. Make a special effort to provide the best quality of play experiences you can. If you don't have a lot of equipment or resources, consider borrowing from a toy library or individual families who might be willing to loan things for a session.

Consider some of the following different types of play: play dough (see recipe below); junk modelling; sand tray or water play (these don't have to be in large quantities – small bowls with suitable floor covering and careful supervision will be as interesting as large specialist stands and trays); sponge painting; a slide, rockers, or ride-on toys; different types of building blocks; jigsaws; crayons and paper; home corner with dressing up box, dolls, play cooker and tea sets; small cars, trucks and other small play vehicles; a farmyard and set of animals.

Play dough recipe

Multiply up these proportions to make larger amounts of dough: children love to have generous quantities to play with.

2 cups plain flour
1 cup salt
2 cups water
food colouring
10g cream of tartar
30ml cooking oil

Mix together in a strong (but not your best!) saucepan over a low heat, until the mixture comes away from the pan sides. Allow to cool; then knead well.

For variety:

•Add perfumed hand lotion to give a sweet smell.
•Add glitter for a special occasion.
•Add rolled oats for an unusual texture.

Game time

5-10 mins

Choose and play

Sit in a circle, placing a box of musical instruments in the centre. Let each child in turn (or in pairs, if they are less confident) come into the middle and choose an instrument to play. While they do that, everyone else sings to them, using the tune 'Peter hammers with one hammer'.

Matthew plays the jingle bells, jingle bells, jingle bells,
Matthew plays the jingle bells, let's all play with him.

During the last phrase, all pretend to play along with the child.

Making time

4-5 mins

Look at me

You will need: *A4 coloured card, 14 x 10 cm pieces of mirror card, copies of Psalm 139:13,14 printed in a large font, hole punch, wool, inkpad or paint, sticky shapes to decorate.*

Make a hanging mirror picture to remind the children of Psalm 139. Help the children to stick the words of the psalm and mirror card onto stiff A4 card. Punch holes at the top of the card and thread wool through to make a hanging picture. Allow the children to decorate the border of the picture with fingerprints and/or sticky shapes. Ask them to look into their mirrors to see someone very special!

Yes Mickey, he can.

Can he see me when I hide under my bed covers?

Yes Mickey, even when you're hiding.

Can God see in the dark Jean?

He can see in the dark and in the daylight. He knows where you are, what you're doing, what you are thinking and he even knows what is going to happen when you grow up! God knows everything. In fact, he knows that we are talking about him right now.

Is he listening to us Jean?

Yes he is Mickey. Shall we speak to him?

Yes, let's!

Dear God, thank you that you know all about us. Thank you for making each one of us different. Please help us to grow up to be the special people you want us to be.

Rhyme time

God is with me
Vary the third line of this rhyme (thinking, playing, eating). Ask children for suggestions for further verses (swimming, singing, sleeping). Repeat your version and this time, encourage the children to add simple actions to go with each verse.

God is with me,
God is everywhere,
Whatever I am doing,
God is always there.

God is with me,
God is everywhere,
When I am walking,
God is always there.

Song time

These two easy-to-learn songs assure children of their 'specialness' and how we are all made by God.

Who is it?
Sing this song, to the tune of 'Frère Jacques', sitting in a circle so that everyone can be looking for the person described. Change the description and the child's

name each time to fit your children, trying to be as individual as you can eg, blond hair, rosy cheeks, a cheeky smile, a loud laugh.

Who's got *blue* eyes? Who's got *blue* eyes?
Can you see? Can you see?
God made… *(Name.)* special,
God made… *(Name.)* special,
And so are we, and so are we.

God made you
Sing to the melody of 'Bobby Shaftoe'. Ask the children to suggest different actions for further verses.

Clap your hands and
wiggle your fingers, *(x 3)*
See how well God made you.

Wave your arms, and nod your head…

Touch your nose and blink your eyelids…

Touch the floor then reach up high…

Pray time

God knows and cares
Encourage the children to join in with the repeated words.

When I stand up and walk upstairs,
God knows and he cares.
When I go out or stay at home,
God knows and he cares.
When I go to play with my friends,
God knows and he cares.
If I get up to see the sun rise,
God knows and he cares.
If I'm up late and the dark scares,
God knows and he cares.
Before I was born, God knew I was there,
God knows and he cares.
As I get bigger God watches me still,
God knows and he cares.
Wherever I go, whatever I do,
God knows and he cares.

Extra time

•Make a group height chart against a door or wall using wallpaper. Keep a record of the children's heights, each month.

•Ask parents and carers to bring photographs of their children as babies. Make a display of them all at a height where children can see them. Help them to identify who is who and talk about how each child has changed and grown.

Adults too

In the days of reality television, a psalm that tells of a God who sees and knows everything in the past, present and future might seem a little unnerving to many adults. Even the psalmist found it 'far above me' (Psalm 139:6). But God's 'knowing' is rooted in love and compassion for those he has created. It is not about knocking people down, but building them up to become the people God intended them to be. His image is within us all, regardless of what we believe.

Look for the goodness of God in the adults in your group. Give them a copy of this psalm to take home and read. If you know any of them are going through difficult times, the poem called 'Footprints' tells of a person reflecting on difficult times in their life's journey. (You can often find it on bookmarks and cards in a Christian bookshop.)

Top tip

Storing toys and equipment for play can be a nightmare. Consider the following:

•Use boxes with lids so that you can stack easily.

•Add carefully measured shelving to cupboards to fit your storage containers and optimise available space.

•Fix pegs up to hang lightweight equipment and drawstring bags.

•Label shelves and containers clearly so that others can help pack away.

•Involve carers in regular sorting and cleaning of toys and equipment.

ACTIVITY PAGE:
The photocopiable activity page for this outline is on page 60

For your notes:

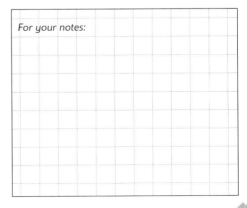

Stephen

Acts 6:1–8

Play time

Waiter, waiter

You will need: child-sized tables and chairs, tablecloth, play tea set and cutlery, aprons, trays, tea towels, pretend food (optional).

Set aside an area as a restaurant so that some children can dress up as waiters and set the table, take orders and serve the food. Others can sit at the table and be the customers. You will probably find that the children make up their own game and choose their own roles.

Veggies!

You will need: a large bowl of water; aprons; small scrubbing brushes; peas in pods; root vegetables – potatoes, parsnips, carrots; toy oven or cardboard box; pots and pans (optional).

Show the children how to shell peas and let them have a go. Make sure all the children have aprons on and are supervised at all times. Let them scrub the other vegetables clean in the water. The children can also pretend to cook them for the restaurant with a toy oven or cardboard box.

Clay fun

You will need: clean plastic mats, sweet clay. (Blend together ½ cup margarine; 3 g salt; ½ cup golden syrup, 5 ml vanilla essence. Then add 450 g caster sugar. Knead till smooth. Add more sugar if necessary to make pliable 'clay'.)

Put out some plastic mats with a ball of sweet clay on each. Make sure the children wash their hands, then allow them to play with the clay. Show children how to make a long worm-shape and then help them coil it up to make a basket. Encourage them to make balls of clay to put into the basket as apples.

Game time

Let's help Stephen

You will need: a basket of vegetables (real or pretend), 'soup pot' (bucket or bowl).

Line the children up in single file (with a large group, have more than one game happening at the same time, or they will get restless). Place a 'soup pot' on the floor in front of them. Explain that Stephen is going to make soup for all the poor people and we're going to help him by fetching the vegetables. Place the vegetable basket at the other end of the room. When the leader shouts, 'Let's help Stephen!' the first child runs (walks, crawls, hops, etc) to the basket, picks up one vegetable and runs back and drops it in the soup pot. The next child repeats these actions, until the basket is empty and the pot is full.

Making time

What a treat!

You will need: paper plates, two small cakes or plain biscuits per child, icing, decorations (small sweets, hundreds and thousands, etc), blunt knives, plastic film or paper for wrapping food.

Give the children the opportunity to make a treat for their parents or carers and then serve it to them.

Remember to consider any dietary needs the children may have. Show the children how to ice the cakes or biscuits and then decorate them. Let them serve one of their creations to their parent or carer or cover it in food-wrap to take home. The other item is for the child to eat.

Meal for one

You will need: magazine pictures of food, glue, glue spreaders, paper plates.

Allow the children to choose their meal from the pictures of food and glue it to the plate.

Story time

Helping and serving

You will need: a large white apron, tea towel, plate of small fruit or fruit slices (strawberries, sliced apple, raisins – check beforehand about possible allergies).

Ask a leader to sit the children in a semi-circle. Dress up as a waiter and serve the fruit to the children. Pause while they enjoy eating it. Introduce yourself as 'Stephen' and tell your story.

Hello, everyone. My name is Stephen. Did you enjoy the fruit? You did! I'm so glad because I really enjoyed washing it and serving it to you. I love doing things for other people. That's why the people in the very first church chose me to do a special job. I'll tell you about it.

Jesus had gone to live with his father in heaven. His twelve special friends stayed behind and told everyone about him. Soon more and more people believed in Jesus and became Christians. They became the first 'church'. Some of these people were very poor and hungry, so Jesus' special friends gave them food every day. We all shared what we had and helped each other.

Soon there were so many people that it was hard to give everyone their fair share of food. Some people thought that they were not getting enough food. Others argued – 'It's not fair…' 'You've got more than me…'

Jesus' special friends had to sort out all the food. They had to feed all the poor people. They didn't have time to pray. They didn't even have time to tell people about Jesus. So they called us together and said, 'You must choose seven men to look after the poor people so that we have time to pray and tell people all about Jesus.'

We all thought that this was a good idea. Someone said, 'Stephen, would you like to look after the poor people?'

I said, 'Yes!'

No more hungry tummies! I was so happy! Now I could make sure all the hungry people had enough to eat. The mummies were happy! The children were happy! Everybody was happy!

Rhyme time

Happy helpers

Act out being members of the early church and serve one another.

Some mummies and their children
   had very little food,
(Cup hands, shake head.)
Some mummies and their children
   had very little food,
Some mummies and their children
   had very little food,
So the people in the church
   gave them help.
(Hold hands out, flat palms up.)

They chose seven men to
   serve out the food…
(Giving out action.)
Yes, the people in the church
   gave them help.

Now everybody's happy as
   they care for one another…
(Hugging action.)
With the people in the church giving help.

Song time

God's little helpers

Sing to the tune of 'Did you ever see a lassie'.

I'm God's special little helper,
   his helper, his helper.
I'm God's special little helper,
   his helper am I.
As Stephen helped all, I'll try too
   though I'm small.
I'm God's special little helper,
   his helper am I.

I'm God's special little helper,
   his helper, his helper.
I'm God's special little helper,
   his helper am I.
I'll help Mum and Dad,
   and they will feel so glad.
I'm God's special little helper,
   his helper am I.

I'm God's special little helper,
   his helper, his helper.
I'm God's special little helper,
   his helper am I.
I'll help everyone,
   till their work is all done.
I'm God's special little helper,
   his helper am I.

Also:

'Helping friends', *LSS* p77; 'Helping friends', *LACH* p91; 'Helping', *LACH* p92.

Pray time

Dancing dusters

You will need: a duster or tea towel for each child, lively praise music.

Seat children comfortably and talk about how they can help and serve others even though they are not grown up like Stephen. What could they do to help at home? Be realistic here. Hand out the dusters. Tell the children that they are going to dance with them to show God that they want to work and be his special helpers. Play the praise music and encourage them to wave their dusters and dance in time to the music.

Ask the children to say this prayer with you:

'Dear Father God, please help me to be a good helper. Thank you.'

Extra time

•Have a food collection: encourage everyone to bring contributions for those in need in your community.

•Give the children an opportunity to serve by bringing furniture polish and dusters, and asking them to help polish the furniture in the room (very close supervision required).

•Make table place mats by decorating sheets of thin A4 cardboard and laminating them before use.

•Make pictures using vegetable or fruit-shaped templates. Make potato prints.

Adults too

Here are some ways to follow Stephen's example, showing God's love by helping and serving others. Pray that God will show who needs help and how to help.

•If any of your parents or carers tells you about a problem, ask if there is anything that you or the church community can do to help.

•If a parent or carer is in hospital or ill, offer to organise people from your church to help prepare meals for the family.

•If a parent or carer has transport problems or difficulty walking, offer to take them shopping or do it for them.

•Can you, as a group, offer to help each other with gardening, babysitting, ironing?

Chat with the adults over a cup of coffee and let them know that you enjoy working with their children and consider it a privilege. Make sure that they know that they are also special and important to you. Look out for any opportunities to serve them.

Top tip

Help develop the children's mathematical skills by giving them opportunities to count. Choose different children each week to serve refreshments: they can practise counting how many children are at a table, how many biscuits they will need, how many children want a drink. They must remember to count themselves or there will not be enough.

ACTIVITY PAGE:
The photocopiable activity page for this outline is on page 61

For your notes:

God loves it when I am "me".

Psalm 139

My name

My name is

My birthday is

My age now

My height now

My weight now

Look in a mirror to help you draw a picture of yourself in the frame. Ask a grown-up friend to help you fill in the facts about you.

This is my hair colour.

This is my fingerprint.

The best thing about me is

Stephen was a good helper.

Help Stephen share the food with the hungry people. Draw a line so each person has some food to eat.

Acts 6:1–8

My name

Paul and Silas

Acts 16: 16–40

Play time

Concert time
You will need: dressing-up clothes (preferably shiny and glittery ones), different shoes, hats, wigs and costume jewellery (optional), musical instruments (toy or real), old microphones (or make your own by painting cardboard tubes and attaching a sponge ball to one end), a stage (make one with wooden boxes or a long low table).

Encourage the children to have fun dressing up and going on stage. Invite them to use the microphones to sing their favourite songs. An audience will probably gather – some children will line up chairs in rows to sit on, or sit on the floor to watch the show and applaud. Some children will just enjoy dressing up.

Paper chains
You will need: strips of brightly coloured paper approximately 20 cm long and 3 cm wide – several per child, glue sticks.

Show the children how to make paper chains: apply glue to one end of a strip of paper and overlap the ends to make a circle. Thread another strip through this circle and overlap the ends to make another circle. Repeat this process to make a chain. Younger children will need help to do this. Allow the children to play with the chains or to use them to decorate the room.

Make a building
You will need: building blocks, play people.

Invite the children to build a prison or building of their own choice. Encourage them to build something of their own design. Some may get side-tracked and not make buildings at all. Don't worry if they do this, because they are being creative and having fun. They will enjoy playing with the play people in the buildings and some children might make furniture as well.

Game time

Bag of rhymes
You will need: a drawstring bag with small objects that children will associate with familiar nursery rhymes or songs, eg a plastic mouse, toy bus, an orange, music.

Pass the bag around the circle as the music plays. When the music stops, the child holding the bag takes out an object and holds it up. He identifies the object and then sings or recites a relevant song or rhyme. For example, if a child finds a mouse they could recite 'Hickory Dickory Dock' or 'Three Blind Mice'. Repeat several times, so other children can have a turn. If the child cannot think of a rhyme, the whole group can make suggestions. If you are working with very young children, let the whole group say the rhymes each time.

Making time

up to 20 mins

In and out
You will need: a card or plastic box with separate lid for each child, craft knife, sticky tape, drinking straws, card copies of Paul and Silas from Activity page 66, scissors, crayons, Blu-tack.

Beforehand cut out a large rectangle from each box lid. **Be safe!** Keep the craft knife

well out of the children's reach! Help the children tape straws across the hole to form prison bars. Colour and cut out Paul and Silas. Turn the boxes sideways and affix Paul and Silas to the back of the box with Blu-tack. Put the lid (prison door) in place. The children can use it to retell the Bible story.

Story time

Singing in prison
Use a rat puppet to tell the story. Make a nose from a semi-circle of card wrapped round to make a cone, tape on two cardboard ears and add some drinking straw whiskers. Operate the rat by putting your first two fingers into the cone and gripping with your thumb. Hide it behind your back and encourage the children to squeak to call your friend Ratty Rat.

Hello everyone. I'm Ratty Rat! Where do you think I live? In a prison. Would you like to hear about the most exciting night ever in my prison?

It all started when two new prisoners arrived: Paul and Silas. They hadn't done anything wrong. They had been telling people the good news about Jesus. Do you know who Jesus is? Yes, that's right, he's God's son. What was the good news? It was that Jesus wants to be our friend – and we can be friends with him for ever!

Some men didn't like them talking about Jesus. 'Lock them up!' they shouted.

The jailer took Paul and Silas into the prison. He fastened their feet between heavy blocks of wood. He used chains to tie them up.

'They won't be able to sleep tonight,' I thought.

I was right – they didn't sleep. But they didn't sit and moan either. They prayed to God and sang songs to praise him. It was wonderful to hear! All the other prisoners (and us rats) were listening to them.

Suddenly, there was an earthquake. The walls in the prison shook! The doors flew open! The prisoners' chains fell off!

The jailer woke up! He thought the prisoners had escaped. But Paul shouted, 'Don't worry! Everyone's still here!'

'Bring lights!' shouted the jailer. He ran to Paul and Silas. 'What must I do to be saved?' he asked.

Paul and Silas told the jailer and all his family about Jesus. And they all became friends of Jesus too. Everybody was so happy!

Next day Paul and Silas left the prison and they carried on telling people about Jesus.

But I'll never forget that night! I wonder if I can remember what they were singing…

'Squeak' a praise tune that the children will know and see if they can identify the song!

Rhyme time

Paul and Silas
Review the story with this rhyme.

Paul and Silas sit in the cold dark prison.
Their backs are very sore
   but the other prisoners listen,
To Paul and Silas singing hymns of praise!
They belong to Jesus
   so they pray to him always.
Paul and Silas feel the prison
   start to shake.
Then all their chains fall off
   in a great earthquake.
Paul and Silas see the jailer full of fear.
'Don't worry!' shouts Paul.
   'We're all still here!'
Paul and Silas tell the jailer what to do:
'Believe in Jesus right away
   and you'll belong too!'

Song time

Praising God
Sing to the tune of 'London Bridge'.

Prisoner Paul is praising God,
Praising God, praising God.
Prisoner Paul is praising God.
Alleluia.

Silas too is praising God,
Praising God, praising God.
Silas too is praising God.
Alleluia.

Prisoner Paul is praying now…
Silas too is praying now…
All the doors are opening now…

All the chains are falling off…
Everyone is thanking God…

Also:

'Praise him, Praise him all you little children', *JP* 201
'Jesus loves me', *JP* 140
'Shake those hands', *KS* 294
'We don't sing songs just for ourselves', *KS* 355

Pray time

Pretzel prayers
You will need: a twisted pretzel for each child (be aware of allergies)

Talk about Paul and Silas praying when they were in prison – the Bible tells us they were praising God. Ask the children about their prayers. Guide the discussion so that they realise that God wants them to praise him and pray all the time, especially when they are frightened or sad.

Show the children a pretzel and explain that when pretzels were first made they were supposed to look like children whose arms were crossed in prayer. Suggest the children fold their arms like pretzels and repeat a simple prayer after you.

Please be with me,
When I'm happy,
When I'm sad,
When things are good,
When things are bad,
Dear God, I love you.

Give each child a pretzel and let them eat it.

Extra time

•Make simple musical instruments such as shakers, drums and blowers. See *Let's All Clap Hands*, published by SU, ISBN 1 85999 528 4, pages 69 and 77 for some exciting ideas.

•Provide percussion instruments and encourage the children to enjoy playing along with their favourite praise music.

•Record the children singing as a group or individually. They will enjoy hearing themselves.

Adults too

Paul and Silas sang and prayed in prison – and the gospel spread. Song is still a wonderful way to tell people about Jesus today. Why not organise an outing to a Christian concert for the parents and carers? (Can your church fellowship offer a babysitting service too, with suitably qualified volunteers?) If there aren't any Christian concerts on offer, suggest that your church organises one. This may be done by asking popular Christian singers to participate, but you will have to book them well in advance. Or, ask the people in your church with singing, acting and musical talents to perform and help to put together a programme. Perhaps it would be possible to work with other churches in the area so that you can pool your talents and resources? Whatever you do, surround it in prayer from beginning to end.

Top tip

When you ask the children questions, accept all responses. If a child gives a 'wrong answer', do not dismiss it lightly or belittle the child. Build self-esteem by letting the speaker know that their input is important to you – listen very carefully and try to apply something from it. If you cannot use the answer in this way, still make a point of thanking the child for contributing.

ACTIVITY PAGE:
The photocopiable activity page for this outline is on page 66

For your notes:

Paul and Epaphroditus

Philippians 2: 25–30; 4:18

Play time

 no limit

Post office fun
You will need: a counter (balance a plank of wood across two boxes), toy till, telephone, lots of old envelopes, paper, crayons, rubber stamps, ink pads, gummed paper, scissors, post box, postie's hat, bag for letters.

Help the children set up the post office and let them have fun playing in it. They will enjoy writing letters and posting them. Ask them who the letters are for and then write the name on the envelope. Let the children choose a postie to empty the post box and put the letters into a shoulder bag. They will have fun going around the room delivering the post.

Have the following activities available:

Stamping – set out rubber stamps and ink pads and let the children stamp all over their paper.

Writing letters – set out sheets of paper, old envelopes and crayons so that the children can 'write' letters and draw pictures, and then fold them and put them into envelopes.

Making stamps – let the children cut out their own postage stamps from coloured gummed paper, draw on them with felt-tip pens and then stick them on to envelopes.

Posting game
You will need: four cardboard boxes each with a slit to post cards and a picture of a family member stuck on, cards with pictures of suitable gifts for family members eg, silk scarf for mum, doll for sister (cut out pictures from magazines and paste them on to thin card).

Shuffle the present cards and place them face down in a pile. The children take turns to pick up the top card, decide which member of the family would like the gift and then post the card in the appropriate box.

Game time

 10 mins

Take a letter
You will need: a letter in an envelope.

Sit the children in a circle. Choose one child to be Epaphroditus walking around the outside of the circle with the letter as everyone chants:

'Paul wrote a letter to the church,
Epaphroditus took it.
He dropped it once,
He dropped it twice,
He dropped it three times over.
One of you has picked it up
And put it in your pocket.
It wasn't you, it wasn't you...'

Epaphroditus drops the letter behind a child and all say, 'It was you.' This child jumps up, picks up the letter and becomes Epaphroditus for another round. The first child takes their place in the circle.

This is complex enough for younger children: older ones will enjoy chasing round the circle and back to the vacant space – but keep the game light-hearted.

Making time

 5-10 mins

Satchels
You will need: a thin brown cardboard, satchel template (enlarged and copied on to the brown card, if possible), scissors, crayons, glue, decorations (pieces of fabric, buttons, etc), scissors, long strips of material to make carrying straps, chocolate or toy money.

Let the older children cut out the satchel templates. Have some already cut for younger children. Fold up the bottom section and staple or glue sides together before folding over the top part. You could punch holes in the sides for older children and help them to thread needles and sew the sides together. Add some

decoration and a long strap made from a strip of card, ribbon, or cord. Give each child a chocolate or toy coin to put in the satchel.

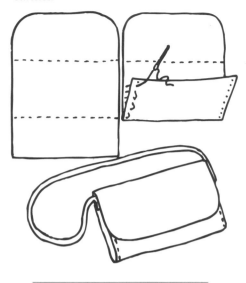

Story time

 10 mins

Paul's letter
You will need: a letter written as a scroll and tied up with rough string.

Ask a helper to seat the children comfortably. While they are waiting for you, they can learn how to say 'Epaphroditus'! Run into the room waving the scroll. Be very excited and happy! Say:

I'm so happy! I want to run and jump! I want to skip and dance! Epaphroditus has come home again! Paul has sent him back home to us.

Look! Epaphroditus brought a letter from Paul. *(Hold up the letter.)*

We heard that Paul was in great trouble – he was in prison for telling people about Jesus. He needed money. We decided to send Paul a present to help him, so we collected lots of money. Epaphroditus took it to him. Let's read Paul's letter.

(Undo the scroll and pretend to read from it.)

Paul and Epaphroditus are such good friends. Paul says that they really enjoyed being together. Epaphroditus helped Paul with his work telling other people about Jesus. Paul says Epaphroditus worked very hard. Paul says Epaphroditus is very brave!

Oh, look! *(Read scroll.)* Paul says that Epaphroditus was upset because we had heard that he was very sick. *(Look up.)* That's right, we did hear he was sick and we were all very worried! Paul says that Epaphroditus was so sick that he nearly died, but God made him better again! He's really well now! I'm so glad. *(Read scroll.)*

Paul wants us to give him a big welcome. Let's all shout, 'Welcome,' and cheer for him.

Welcome! Three cheers for Epaphroditus. Hip, hip, hooray! Hip, hip, hooray! Hip, hip, hooray.

(Encourage everyone to join in with cheering.)

I wonder if we sent enough money to Paul. Let's see what he says. *(Read scroll.)* He says that he has everything that he needs – in fact, he has more than he needs because we sent him so much money! I'm so glad!

And now I'm going to find Epaphroditus and give him a really big hug – it's wonderful to have him home again. Goodbye, children.

Rhyme time

Paul's letter
Groups of children could act out this rhyme: some as Paul, some as Epaphroditus and some as the welcoming people of Philippi.

Paul wrote a letter,
    a letter to send,
A letter to Philippi,
    about a good friend.
He said in the letter
    his friend was to go,
To journey to Philippi.
    Paul thought they should know.

They all read the letter –
    they thought it was great.
The people of Philippi
    had not long to wait.
The poor tired traveller
    arrived in the town.
At last he'd reached Philippi.
    He dumped his bags down.

Then 'Hello' and 'Welcome',
    'We're happy you're here.'
The people from Philippi
    were all crowding near.
He couldn't feel lonely,
    he couldn't feel sad.
His new friends at Philippi
    had made him feel glad.

Song time

My special friend
Sing this song to the tune of 'Mary had a little lamb'.

Jesus is my special friend,
Special friend, special friend.
Jesus is my special friend,
And I am his friend too.

I shall always love him so,
Love him so, love him so.
I shall always love him so,
And Jesus loves me too.

I shall always work for him,
Work for him, work for him.
I shall always work for him,
Because I love him so.

Also:

'For he's a jolly good fellow' (traditional)
'Best friends', *LACH* p91
'Helping', *LACH* p92

Pray time

Good friends
Sit the children in a circle and chat about how Epaphroditus was a good friend to Paul when he was in trouble. Talk about ways in which they can be good friends to each other, eg sharing toys.

Choose a confident child to shake a friend's hand or give a 'high five' hand slap. Encourage the child to pray 'Thank you God for … (Add child's name.)' This child can then pass the same greeting to another friend and pray. Offer each child an opportunity to participate. Do not pressurise children who are reluctant to take part. Simply ask another child to continue the round.

Finish this time by praying together:

'Thank you for my friends. Please help me to be a good friend.'

Extra time

• Postman Pat books by John Cunliffe, published by Scholastic.

• Make postcards: draw or collage on to one side of a piece of card 15 x 10 cm. Add a message and address to the other side (real or pretend).

• Use quill feathers for writing (use shaft end) or painting (use other end).

• Make get well cards for a child who is sick.

• Write letters with lemon juice or milk – iron the paper to reveal the 'writing'.

Adults too

Paul wrote letters to the early Christian churches and we can still read and enjoy those letters today. They encourage us and teach us about God and his son Jesus. Follow Paul's example and take the time to write to the adults who bring their children to your group. If someone is going into hospital, write them a letter of encouragement. If someone is going through a difficult time in their life, write them a letter to let them know that you are praying for them and that you are available if they need any help. Write and tell them how much you appreciate their attendance every week. You could add a card or bookmark with appropriate texts, thoughts, poems or prayers – see what is available next time you visit a Christian bookshop. Handwritten letters and messages are very special in this electronic age – use them to make people feel special.

Top tip

Children seldom receive letters of their own in the post. Make each child in your group feel special by sending an occasional letter or card – don't wait for a special occasion, do it any time. Choose patterned or colourful paper and write a short message saying how much you enjoy having them in your group and comment on something that you know they have enjoyed doing recently.

ACTIVITY PAGE:
The photocopiable activity page for this outline is on page 67

Acts 16: 16–40

Copy this page on to card, or stick the pictures on to card before you cut them out. Colour and cut out Paul and Silas. Tape loops of card on the back so you can hold them

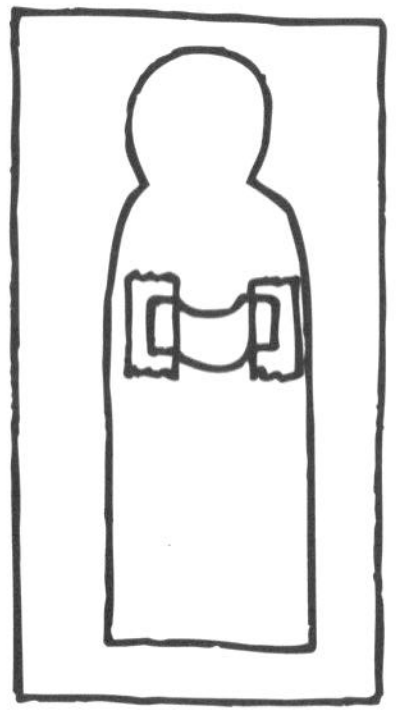

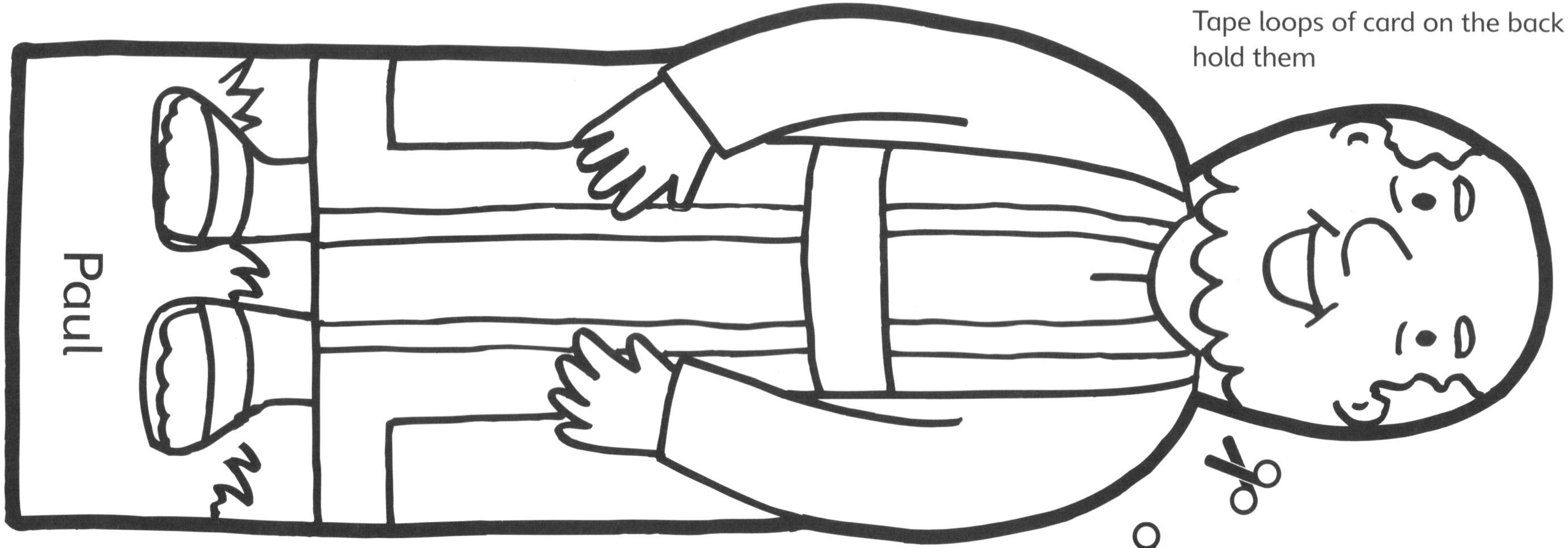

My name

Paul and Silas sang to God.

Paul

Silas

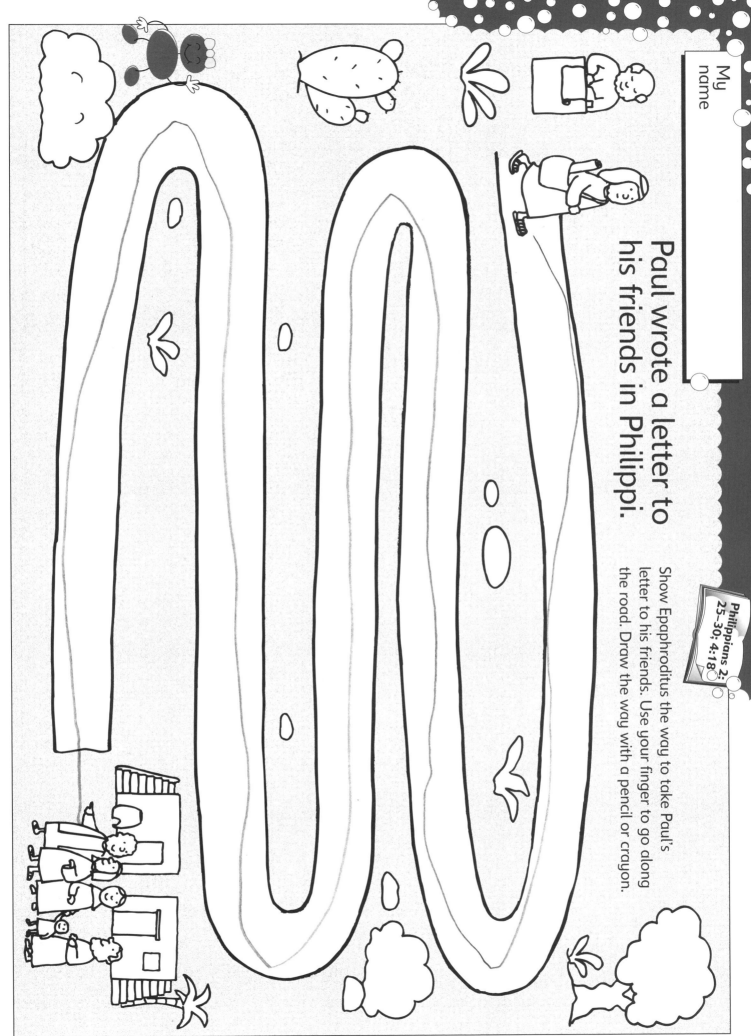

Paul wrote a letter to his friends in Philippi.

My name

Show Epaphroditus the way to take Paul's letter to his friends. Use your finger to go along the road. Draw the way with a pencil or crayon.

Philippians 2: 25–30; 4:18

Paul in trouble

Acts 23: 11–24

Play time

no limit

Build a fort
You will need: large cardboard boxes, cushions, small blankets, clothes pegs.

Children love building and will really enjoy this activity. Suggest they pretend to be soldiers or knights and make a fort. Allow the children to build the fort by stacking boxes and cushions, draping blankets over furniture and pegging them together. Allow them to develop their own creativity and construct the fort to their own design, using their own methods – do not give them instructions! Make sure a leader is supervising at all times to avoid any potentially dangerous construction work. If there is time, allow the children to play in the fort when it is finished.

Hobby horse fun
You will need: hobby horses, sit-and-rock toys.

Set aside an area for the children to ride hobby horses and let them pretend to be soldiers riding their horses.

If you do not have any hobby horses, you could make some as follows: stuff the foot section of an old sock with crumpled pieces of newspaper for the head. Stuff the top of the leg section and push half a wooden broom handle in. Pack more crumpled newspaper firmly around the broom handle to make the neck. Secure the sock to the broom handle with strong elastic bands. Sew two buttons on to the head as eyes and glue on cardboard triangles as ears. Stitch fringing along the back of the neck for a mane.

Night pictures
You will need: chalkboards, chalks.

Set these out, ready for use. Encourage the children to draw pictures of the night,

eg a child sleeping snug in bed or stars in the dark sky. Chalks can be used on dark coloured paper to make pictures to take home.

Game time

10-15 mins

Safe bunnies
All you need: a blanket, whistle.

Spread the blanket on the ground to represent the rabbit burrow. Choose a few children to be bunnies and show them how to hop around like rabbits. Ask the rest of the group and a helper to hold hands and encircle the bunnies to guard them and keep them safe as they move around the room. When the leader blows the whistle, it means that the fox is coming to catch them. (You don't need anyone to be the fox; just pretend.) The children must get the bunnies safely back to the burrow without dropping hands or leaving any bunnies behind.

Choose different children to be bunnies and repeat the game until everyone who wants to, has had a chance to be a bunny. Adapt the game using characters from the Bible story and keep Paul safe.

Making time

15-20 mins

Shiny shields
You will need: cardboard shields, strong cardboard strips, wide adhesive tape, aprons, PVA glue, shiny collage materials, eg sweet wrappers, tin foil, glitter, sequins.

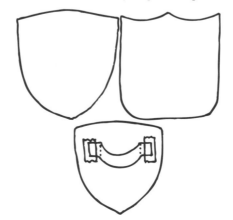

Help the children tape a strip of card to the back of their shields for a handle. Invite them to put on aprons and decorate their soldier's shields with the collage materials, creating their own designs.

Candle pictures
You will need: white paper, white candles, paintbrushes, watery blue paint.

Talk briefly about how candles give light in the dark. Suggest the children use the candles to draw pictures of Paul escaping in the night, riding a horse. Show them how to paint over the page to reveal the hidden picture.

Story time

10 mins

Paul in trouble
You will need: a helper to take the part of Paul's nephew.

Tell the Bible story simply in your own words and then say, 'Here comes Paul's nephew now: he can tell us more about it.' Your helper now 'arrives' and you chat together, something like this:

Paul's nephew: Phew! Uncle Paul is safe now!

You: Safe? Why, what happened?

Paul's nephew: My Uncle Paul was in terrible trouble. I heard that some men wanted to hurt him!

You: Oh no! What did you do?

Paul's nephew: God helped me to save him! I ran quickly to the fort where Uncle Paul was a prisoner. I told him what the men were going to do. Uncle Paul called one of the soldiers and he took me to see the commander of the fort.

You: Who? The man in charge?

Paul's nephew: Yes. I told the commander what I had heard. Uncle Paul was safe in the fort with all the soldiers. But the men wanted to get him out of prison so they could attack him!

You: How could they do that?

Paul's nephew: They were going to tell the soldiers they wanted to ask Uncle Paul some questions. They would ask the commander to let Paul out of the fort to talk to them. But they were going to hide along the road and wait for him. When he came along, they were going to rush out and hurt him. I was really worried about him.

You: Wow, your uncle really was in trouble. What did the commander say?

Paul's nephew: He said 'Ssshh! Don't tell anyone about this.' Then he told his soldiers to get a horse for Uncle Paul to ride and to arrange a guard of hundreds of soldiers.

You: Hundreds of soldiers?

Paul's nephew: Yes, hundreds! Some with spears, some on horses. They kept Uncle Paul safe. They all left the fort at night while it was really dark. Nobody could see them. By the morning Uncle Paul was far away from the men who wanted to hurt him. God had kept Uncle Paul safe!

You: And God used you to help save your uncle! Let's all cheer for God, Paul and Paul's nephew!

Rhyme time

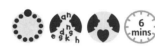

Paul will be safe
During the first verse, the children march on the spot. For the second verse, the children bend their knees and pretend to ride horses.

Left, right, left, right,
Hear the soldiers marching,
Marching through the night.
Left, right, left, right,
Paul will be safe,
When it is daylight.

Clip, clop, clip, clop,
Hear the horses trotting,
Trotting through the night.
Clip, clop, clip, clop,
Paul will be safe,
When the horses stop.

Also:

'My family', *LSS* p85
'Ride a cock horse to Banbury Cross', (traditional)

Song time

All together
Chat about how Paul's nephew helped his

uncle, and people in families today can help each other. Sing to the tune of 'Jingle Bells' (chorus). Be sensitive to any children who do not have a family to care for them.

Thank you, Lord,
Thank you, Lord,
For my family.
I can share the life I live
With those who care for me.
Sisters, brothers, Dad and Mother,
Grans and Grandpas too!
I am glad that God gave me
A family just like you.

March!
Do some marching round the room to music with a strong regular beat. Let children carry drums and other percussion instruments, if available. Songs that fit the marching theme include:

'So we're marching along', *KS* 306
'We are marching', *KS* 350
'Sing a song', *LSS* p16
'I may never march in the infantry' *JP* 101

Pray time

Jesus, here I am
God can and does use anyone he chooses – and that person could be in your group now!

Briefly recap the Bible story, emphasising that God chose Paul's nephew (we don't even know his name!) to do something very important. God chooses children to do special work for him. Illustrate this with a (brief) true story if possible.

Sing together 'Jesus, Jesus here I am' (JR p96) or a similar reflective song, several times. Then include words from the song as you pray:

'Jesus, here we are. Thank you for being our friend. Thank you for loving us. Please help us and show us what you want us to do.'

Be ready to reply gently and positively to any child who responds to this activity.

Extra time

• Stick self-adhesive stars onto black paper to make a night sky.

• Free play: toy fort and plastic soldiers.

• Beat drums, clap and/or march in time to this chant:

March and praise him,
March and praise him,
God is always faithful.
March and praise him,
March and praise him,
There's no one like God!

Adults too

Families are very important to God – he made a wife for Adam and even sent his own son, Jesus, to live in a family here on earth. He knows that we all need to be part of a loving, caring family that will help and encourage us when we need it.

Decades ago families were generally large, with many relatives ready to step into the breach when sickness or disaster struck. Today families are often small and isolated – there are many single parents struggling to look after their children.

Can you plan some events and functions which build family relationships? What about a 'bring and share' lunch after church, a family picnic or barbecue and games afternoon or try the family fun day event on pages 90–91?

Be sensitive to those who have no extended family to help them. Be friendly and hospitable, make them feel welcome and let them know that the people in the church would love them to be part of the church family. Ask God how you can show them that you care.

Top tip

It is a good idea to have several options available at Play time so that the children can choose their own activities and change to others if they want. This helps them to learn how to make choices – a very important life skill. Children with shorter attention spans are less likely to get restless as they simply move on to another activity when they get bored or tired.

ACTIVITY PAGE:
The photocopiable activity page for this outline is on page 72

Paul at sea

Acts 27:1 – 28:15

Play time

15 mins

Water play

You will need: aprons, play people, water troughs with EITHER toy boats (or objects that float, eg polystyrene trays, margarine tubs, pieces of wood) OR whisks and washing-up liquid.

Make sure this activity is closely supervised to avoid accidents. Put aprons on the children and encourage free play with the boats and play people in the water troughs. If boats are not available, encourage the children to make their own using the materials above. OR add washing-up liquid to the water and allow the children to make a storm of waves and foam using whisks.

Sing and dance along with nursery songs like 'A sailor went to sea', 'Row, row, row your boat' and 'The big ships sail'.

Sandy dough

You will need: sandy dough, yoghurt pots or sand moulds, shells, small flags.

Make a batch of dough before the children arrive by mixing and then kneading together:

2 cups of sand
4 cups of flour
4 tablespoons of cream of tartar or alum
4 tablespoons of cooking oil

Encourage the children to mould and shape this unusual dough. They will experience the gritty texture of sand on the beach. Use yoghurt tubs as moulds to make sand castles and then decorate the castles with shells.

Patterns in the sand

You will need: baking trays, sand.

Pour a layer of sand into each baking tray and then invite the children to use their fingers to draw pictures or make patterns in the sand. Children enjoy doing this as they can make the sand smooth again and make as many pictures as they wish.

Stick puzzles

Make puzzles by laying between eight and ten flat craft sticks side by side on a strip of tape. Draw on a pattern with felt-tip pens. Peel away the tape and mix up the sticks to make a puzzle.

Game time

10 mins

Musical boats

You will need: a large blanket, a cushion for each child, music (use a tape of ocean waves if available).

Spread out the blanket and scatter the cushions over the floor. Pretend that the blanket is an island, the cushions are boats and the floor is the sea. Ask each child to sit on a boat and pretend to row. When the music starts, the children jump off their boats and move around the room, making swimming motions with their arms. Remove a boat each time the music plays.

When the music stops, each child must swim to a boat, sit on it and start to row. The child who does not have a boat swims to the island and sits there until everybody is safe on the island.

Making time

15 mins

Splashy shaker

You will need: a clear plastic bottle or jar with a screw-top lid for each child, water tinged with blue (use a drop of food colouring), fish-tank or cactus gravel, gold glitter (gives a sparkling sunlight effect), small shells, funnels, strong glue.

Give the children a jar each and help them to use the funnels to pour in a layer of gravel, some glitter and then water until the jar is half full. Ask the children to choose some shells and drop them into their jars. Smear a line of glue round the

screw-lip of the jar so when the lid is put on it sticks firmly.

Show the children how to turn their splashy shakers sideways and tilt them up and down to make waves and see the sunlight sparkling in the water.

Story time

10 mins

Lost at sea

You will need: a large splashy shaker (see Making time).

Hold the shaker on its side and use it to form waves as you tell the story. Ask a leader to help the children say, 'Splishy, splashy', etc, as they clap or rub their hands to make appropriate wave sounds during the story. A rainstick can also be used.

Our story today is about one of God's special helpers. His name was Paul.

Paul was travelling on a sailing ship with many other people. At first the wind was just right. The waves went, '**Splishy, splashy, splishy, splashy,**' and they reached the port safely. The next day they travelled on another ship. A strong wind blew against them and the waves went, '**Splish, splash, splosh! Splish, splash splosh!**' The ship moved very slowly. At long last they reached a safe harbour.

Paul said, 'Let's stay here for winter. It's much too dangerous to carry on.'

A gentle wind was blowing and the waves went, '**Splishy, splashy, splishy, splashy.**'

The captain said, 'No! I want to go to a better place.' So they sailed on.

Soon a very strong wind began to blow and the waves went, '**Splash! Crash! Smash!**'

For days and days they were caught in a terrible storm. '**Splash! Crash! Smash!**'

It was very dark. They could not see the sun or the stars, so they didn't know where they were! They were lost! They didn't know which way to go. They were very frightened.

An angel came to Paul and said, 'Don't be afraid. The ship will be wrecked but no one will be hurt.' God was going to keep them all safe.

The next morning the ship ran onto a sandbank near an island. The waves kept going, **'Splash! Crash! Smash!'** The ship began to break into pieces. Some people swam onto the sandy beach. Others held onto pieces of wood from the ship and made little rafts to get them to the shore. They all reached the island safely and kind people there looked after them.

God kept Paul and everyone he was with safe when they were lost and helped them to find land.

If you ever get lost, ask God to help you, and he will!

Rhyme time

Just pray
Encourage the children to say the last two lines of each verse with you.

When you are lost,
And don't know where you are,
Don't worry, just pray,
God will show you the way.

When you are lost,
And don't know which way to go,
Don't worry, just pray,
God will show you the way.

When you are lost,
And frightened and scared,
Don't worry, just pray,
God will show you the way.

When you are lost,
Ask God to help you.
Don't worry, just pray,
God will show you the way.

Also:

'Sea praise', *LSS* p13
'God's loving power' *LSS* p81

Song time

All at sea
Sing this story-song to the tune of 'Here we go Looby Lou'. Encourage the children to use their oars: allow plenty of time to sort out which is left and right.

The waves went crashing high,
The waves went crashing low,
The waves went crashing high,
All on a rough stormy sea.
You put your right oar in,
You put your right oar out,
You shake it a little, a little,
And turn yourself about.

God saved the sailors all,
He saved the prisoners too,
God saved the soldiers all,
All on a rough stormy sea.
You put your left oar in,
You put your left oar out,
You shake it a little, a little,
And turn yourself about.

Also:

'Sail little boat', *LACH* p7
'Wide, wide as the ocean', *JR* p72

Pray time

On board
You will need: large shallow container of water; large polystyrene tray; happy face sticker for each child.

Spread the stickers (on their backing) all over the tray and float it on the water. Seat the children around the water tray and talk about how God looked after everyone on Paul's ship when they were lost and in danger.

Explain that we are going to thank God because he is always with us and gives us help when we need it. Teach the children a simple prayer such as:

'Thank you, God, that you are always with me. I can always ask for your help.'

Let each child, in turn, choose a sticker from the boat and say the prayer individually.

Then repeat the prayer all together.

Extra time

•Organise an outing to the seaside where the children can make a beach collage on the sand using seaweed, shells, driftwood and pebbles.

•Finger painting – use blue paints and let the children have fun painting waves.

•Give the children sea shells and glue to make some 3D constructions.

•Make 'pebble pals' using collage materials and paints.

•Mix powder paints with salty water for a sparkling effect.

Adults too

Is there anyone in your group who is going through a tough time like Paul? Perhaps someone in your group is going through a divorce, has financial difficulties, or is finding the demands of childcare hard to manage. Like Paul's shipmates, they may feel without direction, not knowing which way to turn, and also be frightened about the future.

Just as God helped everyone on the ship to get through the storm, he will help us through tough times. Ask God to show you how you can be part of his way to help people around you. Maybe you have battled (or are still battling) through a tough experience. Can you share with others how God was alongside you or brought you through a storm in your life?

Top tip

Craft sticks (ice-lolly sticks) are very useful for puzzles, picture frames, collage work, and 3D constructions. They can be used to make stick puppets, in counting games, to stir paints and as glue spreaders. Craft suppliers may stock sticks in assorted colours; or you can dye plain ones with food colouring.

ACTIVITY PAGE:
The photocopiable activity page for this outline is on page 73

My
name

God kept Paul safe.

Cut out the pictures. Tape them together to make a zig-zag book.

Acts 23: 11–24

1 2 3 4

The boy told Paul.

The soldiers took Paul to a safe place.

A boy heard some men say they were going to hurt his uncle Paul.

They told the captain of the soldiers.

Float or sink?

Put some water in a bowl. Add things one at a time and see if they float on top of the water or sink under it. Try the ideas on this page. Add your own ideas in the empty boxes. Colour above the wavy line if the object floats. Colour under the wavy line if it sinks.

My name

Acts 27:1 – 28:15

stone

Leaf

cup

cork

metal spoon

wood

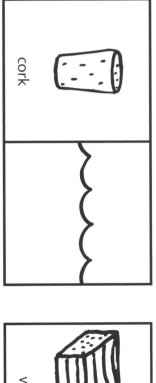

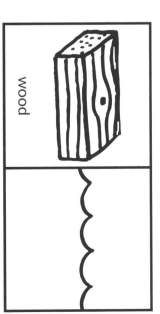

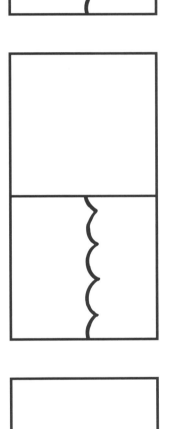

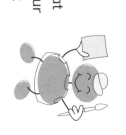

73

Wood

1 Kings 5: 1–12

Play time

no limit

Busy builders

You will need: free play toys, construction toys, tape measure.

Have a selection of free play activities set out for when the children first arrive. Include building blocks, construction vehicles and toy tools for the children to set up a building site. Challenge the children to work together to build the tallest tower or the longest wall and measure their creations.

Display table

You will need: objects made of wood.

Set up an interest table with a variety of items all made of wood. Encourage the children to touch and feel the objects. Take a close look at the grain of the wood and compare the different patterns.

Walkabout

You will need: paper, wax crayons.

Take a walk outside and look for objects made of wood like fences, front doors, benches and so on. Then, look at the trees and think about the different stages involved in turning a tree into a garden gate. Take paper and wax crayons with you and make bark rubbings. Encourage the children to make at least two rubbings, one to display and one to take home.

Explore indoors

If you meet in a church building, why not take the adults and children into the church to explore the building, point out any items that are made of wood. Talk about when your church was built, how long it took and the particular skills and expertise needed.

Sanding wood

You will need: small pieces of splinter-free wood, sandpaper, felt-tip pens.

Provide small pieces of wood for the children to sand. Let them discover how the rough wood becomes smooth as it is sanded. When they have finished sanding, allow the children to draw patterns on their piece of wood with felt-tip pens.

Game time

5 mins

What's missing?

You will need: a wooden tray, wooden objects, cloth.

Place up to ten wooden items on a wooden tray and cover them with a cloth. Let all the children take a good look at the objects and name them one by one. Ask all the children to turn around while you quickly remove one of the items. Let the children guess which has gone. Replace the item and repeat the game, removing something different each time.

Feely bag

You will need: wooden objects, pillowcase.

Place five or six wooden items inside a pillowcase and let each child delve into the bag, feel something and guess what it is. Draw out the items and think about how wood feels hard, but not cold like metal.

Making time

8 mins

Me!

You will need: the initial letter of each child's name cut out of cardboard, bag of clean sawdust (try a pet shop), small twigs and wood shavings, PVA glue.

Give children the initial letter of their name cut from cardboard. Show the children how to cover the letter with glue and then decorate it with sawdust, small twigs and wood shavings.

Sawdust can be coloured with food colouring, or spray paint for a more colourful effect.

Story time

5 mins

Build with wood

You will need: crown and cloak (these can also be used for outline 23), pen or plume, two paper 'scrolls'.

Write Hiram's reply on one of these and give it to another leader beforehand. Tell the story in the costume and character of King Solomon.

Hello everyone! I'm King Solomon and I lived a long time ago in Bible times. Since this is the first time we've met, you really ought to bow or curtsey to me. *(Encourage the children to bow.)* Thank you!

I've decided to build something very special for God. It's going to be a beautiful temple where people can go to pray and to worship him. It will be a bit like one of your churches. But I have a problem; I need some good wood for my workmen to use. I need wood for the doors and wood for the roof beams, wood for the floors and wood for the furniture. The only trouble is we don't have any good wood in my country. I know! I'll write a letter to my friend King Hiram. Hmmm, what shall I say…? *(Encourage the children to help you to write a letter something like this…)*

Dear King Hiram,
I want to build a beautiful temple for God. Do you think that you could give me some cedar wood, please? I know that your men are the best woodcutters and I'll pay whatever you ask.

Love from King Solomon.

(Ask a child to act as postie. Give them the letter and ask them to run once round the group before delivering it to another leader. This leader reads it, then gives the child the second scroll to take back.)

Oh look, here's our postie back again. Do you have a letter for me from King Hiram?

Would someone like to unroll it for me? Let me read King Hiram's answer to you.

Dear King Solomon,
My men will cut the trees down for you. We'll tie the logs together like a boat and float them over the sea to you. Don't send any money. You can pay for the wood by sending food for my men.

Your friend King Hiram.

Well, isn't that wonderful? Now I have all the wood I need to build my temple for God. I'll certainly send King Hiram lots of food for his men.

(Next week/another time), I'll ask one of my men to tell you a little more about how we built the temple.

Rhyme time

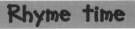

Wood is good!
Repeat this rhyme a couple of times with the children joining in with the response and putting thumbs up on the word 'good'.

Wooden floors and wooden stairs,
Wooden tables with wooden chairs.
We think wood is rather good!

Wooden pencils, wooden toys,
Woodwind instruments
    that make a noise.
We think wood is rather good!

Wooden doors and window frames,
Wooden bricks and special games -
We think wood is rather good!

Wooden things are all about,
'Cos wood is useful, so let's shout...
We think wood is rather good!
Thank you, God, for giving us wood!

Song time

Solomon hammers
Sing the following words to the tune 'Peter hammers with one hammer'. With each verse, let another child join in as Solomon hammering.

Solomon hammers with one hammer,

one hammer, one hammer,
Solomon hammers with one hammer
    all day long.

Solomon hammers with two hammers...

Solomon hammers with three hammers...

Finish with:

Solomon's temple's finished now,
    finished now, finished now,
Solomon's temple's finished now!
    Let's praise God!

Let's build!
Sing these words to the tune of 'The farmer's in his den'.

We'll build a temple with wood,
We'll build a temple with wood,
We'll build it high and build it strong,
We'll build a temple with wood.

Accompany the song with wooden rhythm sticks. There are more verses in the next two outlines.

Pray time

Show and pray
Ask four or five children to volunteer to say a short prayer. Let each child choose an item from your display table or feely bag used earlier in this session. One by one invite the children to stand up show the item and say a one-line prayer, eg: 'Thank you God for... (wooden toys, wooden chairs, wooden bricks, etc.). Allow the children to keep their eyes open while they are praying, so they all know what they are talking about.

Repeat the 'Wood is good' responsive chant from Rhyme time as a prayer.

Extra time

• Use wooden tap-a-shape games to pretend to be busy builders.

• Make simple trees by colouring or painting kitchen roll tubes brown and then sticking strips of green crêpe paper into the top to look like leaves.

• Ask someone to bring in a woodwind instrument to demonstrate how it can be used to play a tune.

• Read *Topsy and Tim: Busy Builders*, by Jean and Gareth Adamson, published by Ladybird, ISBN 0 7214 1935 6, or any similar children's books about construction sites and building.

Adults too

As we hear about the creativity involved in building the temple, why not hold a craft evening where parents can try their hand at one or two different creative activities in a relaxed child-free zone. Parents and carers often have to put their own creativity on hold while they gear all their art and craft activities to pre-school level.

You might want to try linking your craft evening to a particular season. For example: a Christmas craft evening might include making a floral decoration for the centre of the table, icing and decorating a chocolate log and making sugar paste decorations for the top of a Christmas cake. An Easter craft evening might include blowing and decorating eggs, glass painting and making Easter biscuits. Play some gentle background music and have plenty of refreshments available. Many people find it far easier to chat while they are working alongside someone.

Top tip

Save a few trees by using recycled paper and card. Ask the parents and carers to help you provide materials for art and craft by collecting cardboard tubes, scraps of card, etc. Ask those adults who work in offices to look out for unwanted paper that the children can use as drawing paper. Collect leftover rolls of wallpaper and use the reverse side for large posters and collages.

ACTIVITY PAGE:
The photocopiable activity page for this outline is on page 78

For your notes:

Stone

1 Kings 6: 1–14

Play time

no limit

Busy builders

You will need: bricks and construction toys.

Include building bricks in your free play area, plus a selection of construction vehicles and toy tools for the children to set up a building site. Challenge the children to work together to build a house, a church or a school.

Explorers

You will need: adequate supervision.

Take a walk outside. Look out for different stone used in buildings or flagstones, kerbstones and garden statues. Point out that in Bible times buildings were made from stone that had been cut into brick shapes. Today builders make their own bricks by pouring a special mixture into a mould and baking it until it goes hard. Young children will be happy to count everything as stone: pavements, roads and brick walls. Classify any 'stone-type building materials' under this broad umbrella!

Brick rubbings

You will need: paper, sticky tape, wax crayons.

Tape large sheets of paper to a wall and show the children how to rub the side of a wax crayon over the paper until a pattern appears. It should be possible to pick out the shape of several rectangular bricks and the lines of cement in between.

Interest table

You will need: items made of stone, marble, precious stones, etc.

Set up a display table where the children can feel and discuss the texture, weight and purpose of a variety of objects made from different types of stone. You could include: jewellery, paperweights, semi-precious stones, pebbles, gravel and ordinary stones.

Pavement artists

You will need: chalk or cups of water and paintbrushes.

If your meeting place has a safe, outdoor, patio area, let the children draw and colour chalk designs on the ground. Wash away the drawings once the children have gone home. If it's a warm day, give the children a plastic cup of water and a paintbrush to draw water pictures on the paving stones. These drawings will dry quickly in the sun leaving a blank canvas for the next child.

Game time

5 mins

Stepping stones

You will need: paper stepping stones.

Ask the children to sit at one end of the room and lay out a path of stepping stones across to the other end. Explain that you are going to pretend that the floor is a river and that they all need to use the stepping stones to cross the water. Let the children take it in turns to cross from one side of the room to the other. If you include a break for refreshments in your session, why not let the path lead to the drinks and biscuits so that everyone has to use the stepping stones to reach a mini picnic on dry land?

Making time

8 mins

Pet rocks

You will need: a large flat pebble per child, goggly eyes, paint brushes, ready-mix paint in a variety of colours (add some PVA glue to the paint to help it bond to the stones).

Give each child a pebble to decorate as a 'pet rock'. Encourage the children to use their imaginations to create bright fantasy animals, or help those who want

to make a 'real' animal create ladybirds or snails.

Buy some toy 'googly eyes' from a craft shop and stick these in place when the paint is dry.

Stone houses

You will need: house shapes, paint with a little sand mixed in, paint brushes.

Cut simple house shapes out of thin card. Mix up some creamy-yellow paint and thicken the mixture with sand. Help all the children to cover their house shape with paint. While the paint is still wet, draw lines across the house with a pencil or the wooden end of a paintbrush to mark out individual bricks on the house. You may find that the houses need to be left to dry for a day or two before the children take them home.

Story time

5 mins

Stone builders

You will need: a rough apron, gardening gloves, a lump of stone or a brick, a mallet and chisel (adults only!).

Dress up and pretend to be a stonemason as you tell the story. Introduce yourself as someone from a long time ago, who worked for King Solomon cutting stones into bricks for the temple. Pretend to use your mallet each time you say 'Bang! Bang! Bang!' At the same time the children can hammer by knocking a fist onto the palm of their other hand.

Hello everyone! My name is Seth: Seth the stonemason. My job is to cut stones into bricks so that we can use them to build the temple. King Solomon is in charge. He wants to build a very special building where people can come to pray

and to worship God. King Solomon is a very clever king and he knows that it is important to build a beautiful, strong temple. He wants the walls to be so strong that they won't ever fall down. He has asked my friends and me to come and cut the stones into even shapes to make bricks.

Bang! Bang! Bang! We hit the stone with a hammer.

Bang! Bang! Bang! We cut the stone into a brick.

Listen to the noise we make. We have to work far away from everybody else because the other people grumble that our noise gives them a headache and because the king wants God's temple to be a peaceful place. It's very hard work and it hurts our hands too. That's why I'm wearing gloves.

Bang! Bang! Bang! We …

Sometimes we feel tired, but we know that our work is important because we're cutting good strong stones to build the temple.

Bang! Bang! Bang! We …

When we have cut lots of stones into bricks, the men come and take the bricks to the temple. When we see our bricks built into big strong walls it makes us feel really happy, because we know that we're helping to build God's temple.

Bang! Bang! Bang! We cut the bricks for God's temple.
Bang! Bang! Bang! It's a very important job.

Rhyme time

Strong walls!
Use the following words to bring together wood (outline 21) and stone to build the temple. Repeat the rhyme two or three times and show the children how to fit an appropriate action to each line.

Solomon built a temple tall,
(Point upwards.)
And decorated it from wall to wall.
(Stretch arms wide.)
He used fine cut stone and polished wood,
(Mime polishing.)
It certainly looked really good.
(Thumbs up.)
The temple was God's special building,

(Use hands to indicate roof over head.)
The people filled it with
    worship and singing.
(Both hands together in prayer and then raised.)

Song time

Let's build!
Revise the song from outline 21, or learn it now, to the tune of 'The farmer's in his den'. Introduce and learn this verse:

We'll build a temple with stone,
We'll build a temple with stone,
We'll build it high and build it strong,
We'll build a temple with stone.

After you have sung the words through once, give some of the children pairs of small stones to carefully tap together and beat out the rhythm while you sing the song again. Repeat the song letting other children take a turn with the stones.

Pray time

Pebbly prayer
Give the children pairs of small, smooth stones to tap together three times every time they respond with the three words 'Thank you God'. Change your voice to suit the size of the stones – loud and firm for great big rocks and a quiet whisper for tiny little stones.

For great big rocks that we can stand on…
Thank you, God.
For pebbles and stones that we can carry in our hands…
Thank you, God.
For tiny little stones in the sandpit…
Thank you, God.
For beautiful precious stones that we can make into jewellery…
Thank you, God.
For stones used to build big buildings…
Thank you, God.

Extra time

•Decorate large stones with sticky shapes or poster paints; then varnish them to make paperweights.

•Sing 'London Bridge is falling down' and mime building it up again.

•Bring in picture and information books about rocks, precious stones and what is under the ground.

•Make models and statues out of clay and then, when they are dry, paint them a creamy colour to look like stone sculptures.

Adults too

Christ the cornerstone
Explain that it is Christians who make up the church, not the buildings. The church is made up of living stones with Jesus as the all-important cornerstone on which we build our lives and our faith. If possible, point out a cornerstone in your building and see how it holds a vitally important position as part of the foundation supporting the walls above. The first cornerstone determines the angle of the two walls that are built from it and thereafter the remaining walls. All the other stones must be in line with this cornerstone. In the same way, Jesus gives direction to our lives as we try to live our lives in line with his teaching. Check out Ephesians 2:20–22.

Top tip

•Encourage the adults and children to treat Story time as a special time. Dissuade the children from playing with toys during this time. You may find that you need to clear the toys away out of sight in order to get the children's full attention. And if parents are inclined to sit at the back and chat then begin with a simple rhyme eg:

When all the children are quiet,
And when all the grown-ups are quiet,
And when you're all sitting comfortably,
Then I'll begin…

ACTIVITY PAGE:
The photocopiable activity page for this outline is on page 79

For your notes:

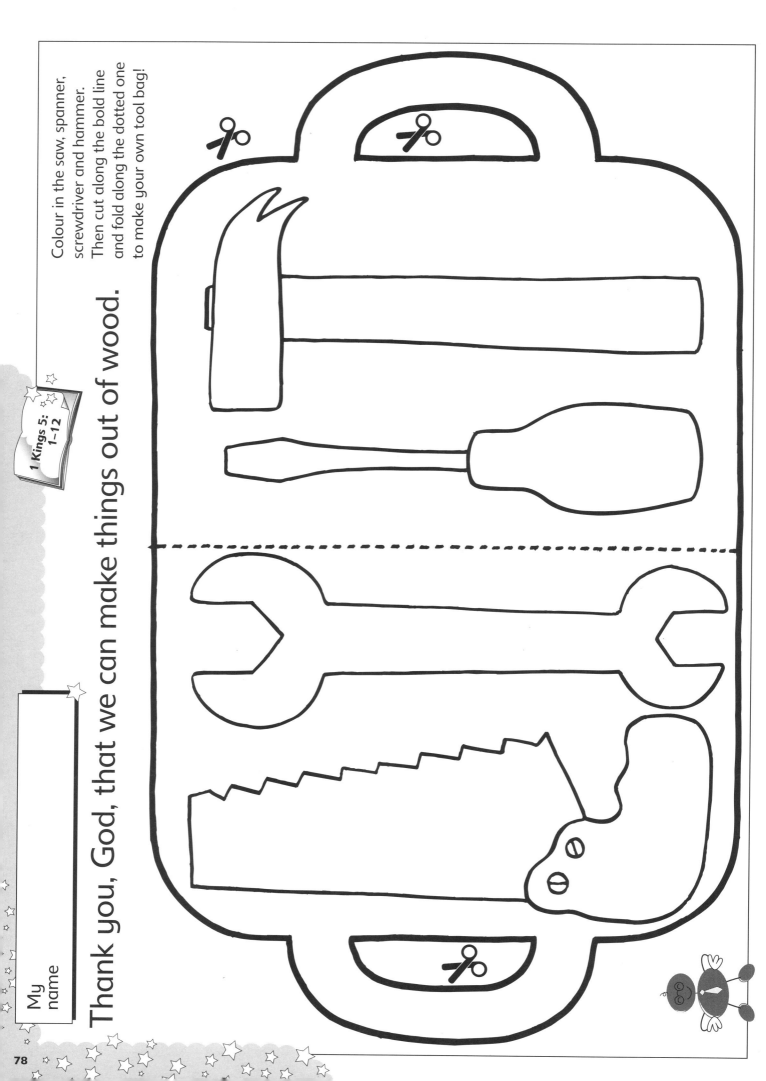

Colour in the saw, spanner, screwdriver and hammer. Then cut along the bold line and fold along the dotted one to make your own tool bag!

1 Kings 5: 1–12

Thank you, God, that we can make things out of wood.

My name

My name

1 Kings 6: 1–14

Thank you, God, for stone to make beautiful things.

Help Solomon finish the temple. Join up the dots to make the stones. Can you work very quietly, like the men who built the walls?

Metal

1 Kings 6: 15–38

Play time

Metal toys
You will need: metal toys, magnetic games, construction kits, etc.

Include several metal-type toys in your free play area, eg toy cars, magnetic fishing games, magnetic letters and numbers with a metal board. Also include bricks, toy tools, construction kits and vehicles to continue the theme of building the temple.

Interest table
You will need: items made of metal.

Create a display of metal objects. You could include: keys, cutlery, jewellery, a toy car, child-safe scissors, coins, a spanner, a grater. Discuss the weight, feel and purpose of each of these objects.

Metallic collages
You will need: plastic lids, dried pasta, PVA glue, gold spray paint.

Use PVA glue to stick assorted dried pasta shapes on to old plastic lids from margarine tubs or similar. Leave the glue to dry. Later ask a leader to take them all outside and spray them with gold spray paint. Let the children watch from the window. When the paint is dry, tape a loop of ribbon to the back of the lid so that the golden collage can be hung up.

Walkabout
You will need: paper, wax crayons.

Take a walk around your building or outside to look for items made of metal. Make sure that you have plenty of adult helpers if you plan to go outside. In the church you might find a brass lectern, a brass plaque, a candlestick, wrought-iron door handles, etc. Outside, look out for cars and bikes, gates and lamposts; drainpipes and metal drain covers. Try making rubbings on flat drain and manhole covers.

Sorting
You will need: wood, stone and metal objects for sorting.

Have a big bag of objects made of wood, stone and metal and three trays. Let the children sort the objects into groups and place them on different trays.

Game time

Metal detectors
Place a chair at either end of your room. Put a plastic spoon on one chair and a metal spoon on the other. Stand in the middle with a box of metal and non-metal items. Draw the objects out of the box one at a time, name them and show them to the children. The children must decide whether they are made of metal or something else and run to the appropriate chair. If any children want to feel the object before deciding, let them do so. Don't worry if the youngest children just follow the crowd: joining in is all part of the game! Ask the children how they decided whether something was metal or not. Draw out that metal is shiny and hard and generally feels cold to touch.

Making time

Beaded bracelets
You will need: a length of wool (approx 24 cm – to fit a child's wrist and tie in a bow) and ten rectangles (5 x 10 cm) of silver foil per child.

Show the children how to wrap a rectangle of foil around their strand of wool and then scrunch it up so that it looks like a bead. Make several beads in this way, leaving the ends of the wool free to tie into a bow. When the wool has ten or so beads, tie it around the child's wrist to look like a bracelet. Some children might prefer to make a bracelet for their mum or a friend.

Foil rubbings
You will need: aluminium foil, Blu-tack, coins and other small items with a raised pattern.

Make patterns by spreading a piece of foil over a textured surface; Blu-tack it to the table to keep it still and gently rub over with a finger.

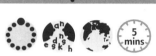

Story time

Golden wonders
You will need: a gold crown, gold chains, gold jewellery and a cloak for King Solomon.

Dress up as King Solomon and tell the children about the gold decorations in the temple (see 1 Kings 6:15–38) from the king's point of view. Tell the story something like this...

Hello again! My name is King Solomon. Do you remember me? God told me to build a beautiful temple, a place where people could pray to him and sing. God said that we should make this temple very special. My friend King Hiram sent us the very best wood to make the doors, floors and roof beams. Then, some of my men cut bricks from huge pieces of stone and these were used to make the strong walls. Finally, I asked some men who knew how to make beautiful things out of gold to come and decorate the temple. Look at my crown, this is made of gold. Look how it shines when the light catches it. And look at this beautiful gold chain. Are any of you wearing something gold? I wanted God's temple to be the most beautiful building in the whole world, so we used plenty of gold. God deserves the very best.

The carpenters made beautiful pictures

of angels, flowers and palm trees out of wood. We covered these pictures in gold. We covered the doors and walls and even the floor in gold. When people walk across the floor it shines like a mirror. It's amazing.

It was hard work building such a beautiful temple. Lots of people had to help and we worked for seven whole years until it was finished! Can you count up to seven? One, two, three, four, five, six, seven years and then it was finished. I stood and smiled and smiled. The sun was shining down on God's wonderful temple. It glittered and glistened. Everyone said, 'This is the most beautiful temple in the whole world.'

'Yes,' I said. 'We have used wood and stone and metal to build a beautiful temple. We built it for God, to show him how much we love him.'

Rhyme time

Marvellous metals

Cover a number of small items in silver foil, which should be moulded exactly around the shape of the object. Try covering a banana, a pencil, a toy car, a plate and a spoon. Let the children identify each item from its shape. Remind the children how Solomon filled God's temple with beautiful things made out of precious metal. Say this rhyme:

We use metal to make a million things,
Like earrings, necklaces
   and golden rings,
Bangles, bracelets and jewellery,
Silver coins and the front door key.

Metal for cars and trucks and vans,
Knives and forks and pots and pans,
Sewing needles, scissors and pins,
Metal bowls and baking tins.

Wrought-iron gates with strong padlocks,
A bronze handle near a brass letterbox,
A stainless steel sink or a shiny kettle,
Thank you, God, for giving us metal!

Song time

Let's build!

Revise or learn the verses about building the temple with wood (outline 21) and stone (outline 22). The tune is 'The farmer's in his den'. Sing the wood verse accompanied by rhythm sticks, the stone verse by tapping pebbles, and the final verse by cymbals and triangles, or pairs of metal spoons, tapped together:

We'll build a temple with metal,
We'll build a temple with metal,
We'll build it high and build it strong,
We'll build a temple with metal.

Divide the group into three and give each group one type of instrument to play during the appropriate verse. Use hand signals to bring them in at the correct time in the style of an orchestral conductor!

Pray time

Prayer collage

You will need: metal objects, backing paper or wallpaper, marker pen, PVA glue, silver foil, metallic gift wrap and sweet wrappers.

Write the words 'Thank you God!' in large outline lettering on to backing paper or wallpaper. Then help all the children to fill in the letters by sticking down scraps of silver foil, shiny metallic gift wrap and sweet wrappers.

Let the children each choose a metal object from the display table or a metal toy to hold. Take turns to say a one-line prayer thanking God for that particular object. The whole group can join in at the end of each line with a loud Amen. Point to the words on the collage as the prayers are said. For example:

Thank you, God, for metal spoons. Amen!

Thank you, God, for metal cars. Amen!

Extra time

•Polish up some dull or tarnished metal.

•Use magnets to test the metal and non-metal objects. Sort out aluminium from steel drinks cans for recycling.

•Make cardboard crowns for King Solomon and decorate them with scraps of foil and metallic paper.

•Invite a musician to come and play a metal instrument.

•March round the room to the music of a brass band.

Adults too

Why not revise this section on building the temple by going into your own church and identifying all the objects made of wood, stone or metal? Tell the children and parents, very briefly, when your church was built and how long it took to build. For those families who do not come to your church services, familiarity with your church building is a step in the right direction. If time allows, go on to explain what happens in a normal church service. Many feel nervous about coming to church because they do not know what might be expected of them. They are worried that they might not know the correct jargon, or are nervous of drawing attention to themselves by standing up or sitting down at the wrong moment. While explaining things to the children, you may be reassuring the adults too.

Top tip

King Solomon knew the importance of giving the very best to God. He expressed this by filling the temple with finest gold, carved wood and hand-cut stone. How can we give our best to God, in our work with very young children? In how we treat them; by having time for them; by showing our love for them; by wiping painty floors and tearful eyes. Give a beautiful gift to God today!

ACTIVITY PAGE:
The photocopiable activity page for this outline is on page 84

For your notes:

Fabric

Acts 16: 11–15

Play time

no limit

Purple play
You will need: red and blue paint, paintbrushes, mixing palettes, aprons.

Give the children red and blue paint. Let them experiment with mixing the two colours together in a palette. Try adding more red and then more blue to make different shades of purple. Often children are just given ready mixed paint, but mixing their own colours helps them to be more creative and to understand how colours combine to make new colours. Give the children paper so they can make some purple pictures.

Collage pictures
You will need: purple collage materials, glue, purple paper.

Cut out scraps of purple paper, card and fabric, and add large purple buttons and ribbons. Give the children some paper (purple if possible!) and let them create a purple collage.

Purple clothes
You will need: purple clothes.

Try and find some purple clothes, perhaps from charity shops. Make simple cloaks from squares of purple material or scarves, and hats from rings of purple sugar paper. Let the children dress up in these clothes.

Purple biscuits
You will need: biscuits, icing sugar, red and blue food colouring, bowls, spoons and blunt knives, purple sweets.

Let the children mix some icing sugar with red and blue food colouring (just use a little). They can then ice some plain biscuits and decorate them with purple sweets. Talk about how red and blue mixed together make purple.

Sorting by colour
You will need: coloured objects to sort.

Have a collection of objects, either all the same, such as buttons, or all sorts of different objects. Ask the children to sort them into different colours. Make sure your collection includes several purple objects. The children could also look round the room for purple toys and objects to add to the collection. Sorting is a useful mathematical skill.

Game time

8-10 mins

Weaving games
Ask the children to stand in a circle and hold hands to make arches. Play 'In and out the dusky bluebells,' where one child weaves in and out of the arches. This child then taps another child on the shoulder, who becomes the new leader, as the two children weave in and out. The line gets longer until there are too few arches to continue.

Ask the children to hold hands in a line. The child nearest the wall puts their hand on the wall. The child at the other end of the line then leads the line through the arch made by the child whose hand is on the wall. The line then goes through the next arch and so on. Sing, 'The big ships sail through the alley, alley o'.

Making time

5-10 mins

Weaving
You will need: paper, glue, purple card, purple wool, hole punch, sticky tape, weaving paper.

Cut parallel slits in a rectangle of paper, leaving a border around the slits – don't cut to the edges. Give the children some strips of coloured paper and show them how to weave through the slits, going under then over. Repeat with another strip but this time go over then under. Keep going with more strips. Push the strips close together and glue the ends down onto the border.

Purple sewing
You will need: purple card, hole punch, sticky tape, purple wool.

Punch holes in pieces of purple card. Tape one end of a length of purple wool to the card and wrap some sticky tape round the other end to stop it fraying. Show the children how to thread the wool through the holes to 'sew' the card.

Story time

7-10 mins

Friends with Jesus
You will need: a large sheet of white paper on a board, thick (non-drip) red and blue paint, paintbrush, palette, beaker of water.

Paint a picture as you tell the story to the children.

Our story today starts off by a river. *(Paint a blue wavy river on the left-hand side of the paper.)* Lots of women used to meet by the river to pray. *(Paint red stick women by the river.)* One of the women was called Lydia. She had a very special job. She sold purple cloth.

So, let's paint Lydia here with her friends. I think she needs a purple dress. Oh dear! I haven't got any purple paint. How could I make purple? *(Mix purple in the palette, adding more red or blue until the children are happy with the shade; paint Lydia in purple.)* Lydia was very rich because her purple cloth was expensive to buy. The dye used to colour the cloth purple had to be collected drop by drop from a type of shellfish! So let's put some of her cloth near her. *(Paint some purple squares.)*

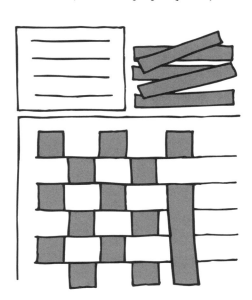

One day, while Lydia and the other women were praying, Paul came along with some other friends of Jesus. *(Paint four blue stick men.)* Paul told Lydia and her friends about all the wonderful things Jesus had said and done. *(Add big blue speech bubble by one man. Mention some stories of Jesus which the children are likely to know.)* And Paul said that Jesus loved Lydia and all the women, and wanted to be their friend.

Lydia was very excited about all they said. She wanted to be Jesus' friend too. She invited all the men to come back to her house to stay. *(Paint a big red house on the right of the page.)* She was a rich woman and had a big house, so she was able to look after Jesus' friends well. 'I can use the money I make selling purple cloth to help Jesus' friends,' she said happily. And every day she loved to listen to more stories of Jesus.

Rhyme time

Busy hands
This is a rhyme about using our hands as Lydia did. Devise your own actions.

With two hands there's lots to do,
Wiggle your fingers, clap hands too,
Count your fingers – one, two, three,
Point up high and wave to me.

Pat a dog or stroke a cat,
Throw a ball, hit with a bat,
Thread a needle, sew in and out,
Hold hands with friends and dance about.

Fasten buttons, do up zips,
Drink your juice and eat your chips,
Paint a picture, cut and glue,
With two hands – so much to do!

Song time

Lydia
Sing this story-song to 'Lavender's blue'.

Lydia works hard, dilly, dilly,
Fabric to sell.
If people buy, dilly, dilly,
She will do well.

Mix red and blue, dilly, dilly,
Purple is seen.

Fit for a king, dilly, dilly,
Fit for a queen.

'See all my cloth,' dilly, dilly,
'Who will come buy?'
Rich people come, dilly, dilly,
Prices are high.

Paul comes to town, dilly, dilly,
Bringing good news,
'Jesus, my friend, dilly, dilly,
Can be yours, too.'

Lydia believes, dilly, dilly,
All that Paul says.
Jesus loves her, dilly, dilly,
Now and always.

'Come to my house,' dilly, dilly,
Lydia says.
'I'll work for God,' dilly, dilly,
'All of my days.'

Pray time

Purple prayers
You will need: *some of the work the children have made in the session.*

Ask the children to bring some of the work they have done in the session (purple paintings, biscuits, weaving, threading) to a display table. Say,

'Thank you God for providing all the materials we needed to make these things. Thank you for…' *(Encourage the children to name some of the materials they have used.)* 'Thank you God for giving us hands to work with and eyes to see. Thank you for giving us the ideas and skills to make these beautiful things. Help us always to work to your glory.'

Extra time

•Have a look in the library for books on colours. Make a display of these.

•Collect purple sweet wrappers. Stick these over the ends of cardboard rolls to make purple telescopes.

•Make lavender bags with dried lavender and circles of thin fabric tied with a ribbon.

•Have purple food and juice at drinks time – blackcurrant juice, grapes, small jam sandwiches.

Adults too

Have a craft evening with different experts demonstrating such things as silk painting, batik and printing on fabric. Perhaps members of the group have skills they could demonstrate. Choose crafts that are fabric-based to fit in with the theme of Lydia. Enjoy being creative.

Have a speaker in to talk about style, personality and colours that suit different people.

Hold an OBNO (outgrown but not outworn!) clothes swap (give out tickets for items donated, hand them in when choosing) or sale (donor labels the item with a suggested price). Have separate tables or racks for adults', children's and baby clothes.

Have a purple evening where everyone wears purple and eats purple food. This could include red wine or blackcurrant juice, purple grapes, plums, purple jelly, black cherry yoghurts and blackberry jam sandwiches.

Top tip

When doing painting, use washable paints and aprons. Old shirts are good for covering the whole child, but paint can get through them, so plastic aprons may be better. Provide shallow containers (eg plastic plates) for children to mix paints on. Have plenty of water to clean the brushes, preferably in beakers with non-spill lids. Have a bowl of soapy water nearby and a towel so that the children can wash their hands straight away.

ACTIVITY PAGE:
The photocopiable activity page for this outline is on page 85

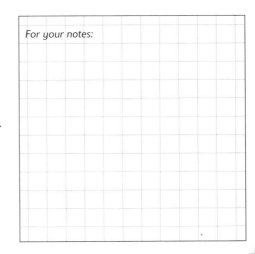

For your notes:

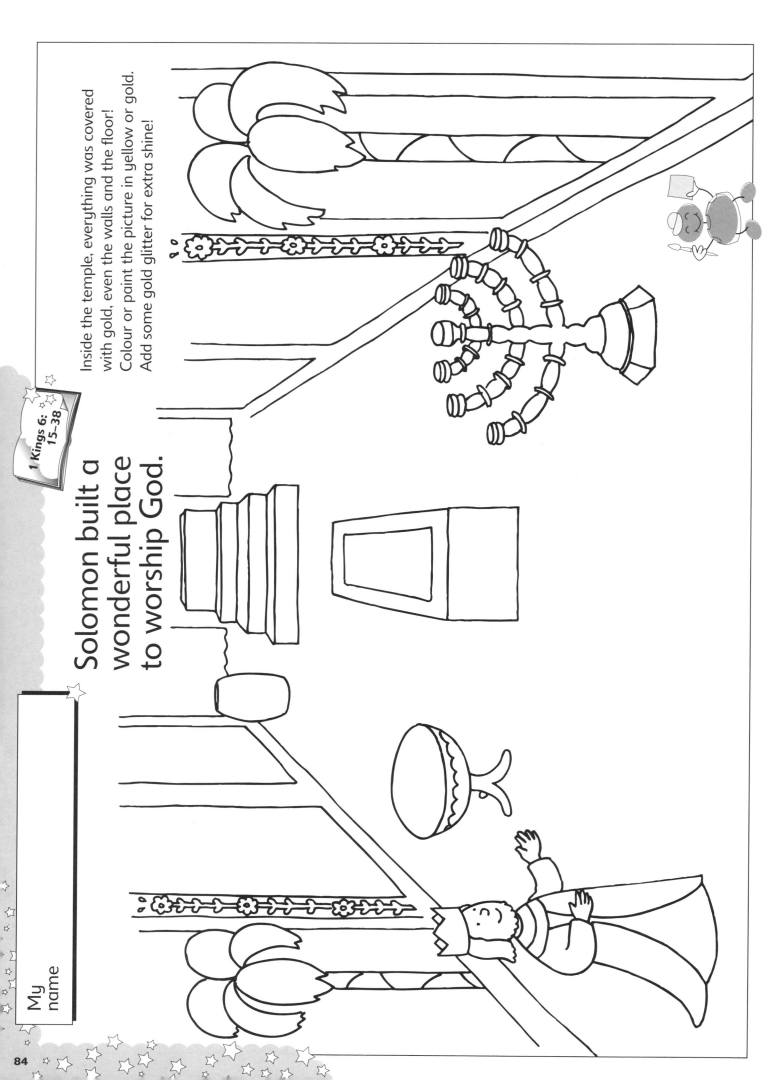

1 Kings 6: 15–38

Solomon built a wonderful place to worship God.

Inside the temple, everything was covered with gold, even the walls and the floor! Colour or paint the picture in yellow or gold. Add some gold glitter for extra shine!

My name

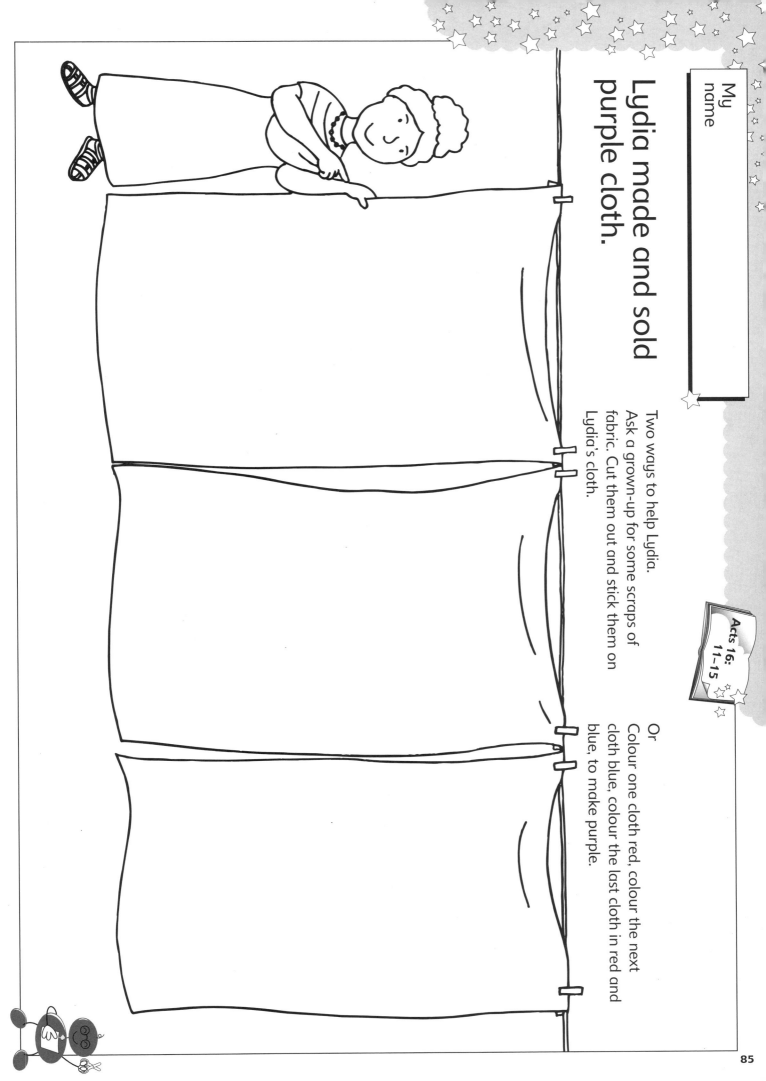

Lydia made and sold purple cloth.

My name

Acts 16: 11–15

Two ways to help Lydia.
Ask a grown-up for some scraps of fabric. Cut them out and stick them on Lydia's cloth.

Or
Colour one cloth red, colour the next cloth blue, colour the last cloth in red and blue, to make purple.

85

Light

Luke 8:16

round the base to cover the lid. Cut flames from the shiny materials and attach these to the top of the candle. Parade round the room so everyone can see your candles lighting the darkness!

Play time

Plants need light
You will need: plants, cress seeds, cotton wool, decorated pots.

If possible, go outside with your group and look at plants growing. If this is not safe or practical, bring a flowering pot plant into the room. Talk about the plant, telling the children how it has grown tall and green. Ask the children if they know what plants need to grow – if it is not offered, tell them it is water and light. Where does the plant get light? Where do we all get light?

Plant some cress seeds on cotton wool in decorated pots. Let the children take them home and watch them grow with light and water. Ask the children to bring them back next time to show each other.

Reach for the sun
Get the children to pretend they are tiny seeds hidden in the dark soil. Ask one child to be the 'sun' and walk among the 'seeds'. Talk about the sun warming the soil and roots starting to grow down into the soil (children stretch out their legs). Then the shoot grows up into the sunlight (slowly stand up) and the leaves open (stretch hands out). Sway in the breeze, grow taller – whatever you can think of!

Shine a light
You will need: a torch, candle, room light, table lamp, simple electric circuit kit.

Have a helper available to show a collection of different lights. How does each one work? Demonstrate one or two items, if you can do so safely. Why do we use or need lights? Can they help us see things or find our way if they are switched off or hidden away?

Make a simple electrical circuit to make a bulb light up. Can the children guess what makes the bulb work? What would make the bulb go out?

Game time

5-10 mins

Walk in the light
You will need: large sugar paper suns, Blu-tack.

A great, fun game to burn off some energy!

Fix the sun shapes to the floor with Blu-tack (have half as many suns as you have children). Play some bright, airy music. When you stop the music, shout, 'bed time!' and the children have to help each other to stand on a sun. Call out encouragingly to the children you see helping the others – the game is about cooperation and helping each other.

Shadow games
Go outside on a sunny day and try jumping on each other's shadows, jumping over shadows, running away from your own shadow.

Making time

4-10 mins

Lighten our darkness
You will need: cardboard tubes, paint, glue, modelling clay, gold or silver paper, coloured cellophane, tinsel, margarine tub lid.

Make 'candles' by painting the tubes. When dry, attach them to the margarine lids with lumps of clay. Wrap the tinsel

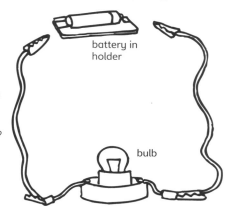

battery in holder

bulb

Stained 'glass'
You will need: clear acetate sheets, felt-tip pens

Let the children make patterns on acetate. When dry, hold the pictures near a window to see the light shine through. Use an overhead projector to display the children's work on the wall.

Story time

7 mins

Shine a light!
You will need: a large flowerpot, small candle (not a tealight), matches/lighter (adult use only), oven gloves, a picture of a New Testament lamp.

Stand together near the entrance to your room. Say, 'Let's pretend it's evening. It's dark outside. We can't see into the room. What shall we do?' Think about what you might do if the electricity wasn't working: you could use a candle, lamp or torch. Look to see where the light comes from in your room (window/sun, artificial lighting). But the light fitting doesn't work without electricity; the candle is no use if it's not lit.

Demonstrate Jesus' word-picture with a small stable candle and large earthenware flowerpot with no drainage hole. Light the candle and carefully place the upturned pot over it. Can you see any light? Remove the pot, using oven gloves.

If the pot fitted well, the candle will have gone out as the flame was starved of oxygen. Light the candle again. This time use the upturned pot as a stand. Can you see the flame now? If possible, dim the room lights to get the full effect of the flame.

Be safe! Let the adults know beforehand what you are going to be doing, and ask them to supervise the children closely, to avoid accidents.

Say this reminds you of something Jesus said. He told stories so we could know what God is like. One day Jesus told his friends, 'When you use a light, you let it shine out. You don't hide it away or put something over the top of it. It's no use then. Lights need to light up!'

Show a large picture of the sort of lamp Jesus would have used. (See *How to Cheat at Visual Aids: The Collection,* published by SU, ISBN 1 85999 500 4.)

Sing a song together based on these Bible verses:
'This little light of mine' (adapted) *KS* 343
'This little light of mine' (trad) *JP* 258
or 'You never put a light' *KS* 398.

Rhyme time

Safety matches!
Help children think 'safety first' by memorising this little rhyme.

Matches, matches, do not touch!
They can hurt you very much!

Lights in our lives
God gives the brilliant sun,
To light up all our lives,
Shining in the daytime,
Life and warmth to give.

God gives us moon and stars,
To light up all our lives,
Shining in the night-time,
Gentle light to give.

God gives us our friend Jesus,
To light up all our lives,
Shining on day after day,
Love and light to give.

Also:

'A light for you', *LSS* p77

Song time

Sunshine!
Chant to the tune or rhythm of 'I'm a little teapot'.

I'm the glowing sunshine,
    yellow and bright,
I light the daytime, chase away the night!
When the rain comes pattering,
    hear me shout:
Look, a rainbow is about!

Sky lights
Sing to the tune of 'Three blind mice'.

Sun is nice, sun is nice,
So is the moon, so is the moon!
God made them both to give us light,
They help us see in the day and the night,
Did you ever see such a beautiful sight,
As sun and moon?

Pray time

Shine on us
Sit the children in a circle, and put a light in the centre (torch, table lamp: take care with trailing flex). Darken the room a little by pulling curtains or turning off room lights.

Lead this responsive prayer with everyone joining in the refrain, 'Shine on us, God'. Learn and practise this first.

As we see the light shining, we are thinking about the way you are the light in the darkness, just like this lamp.
Shine on us, God.
You show us the way to go, and make sure we don't get lost.
Shine on us, God.
Your light keeps us warm, like the light from the sun.
Shine on us, God.
Your light brings us happiness, like the candles on a birthday cake!
Shine on us, God.

Extra time

•Sing and move to 'I reach up high', *KS* 171.

•Ask the children how many things they can think of that give off light.

•Make shakers. Cover them in yellow and gold paper and sequins – make them very glittery! Play the instruments, dance and sing – and make a joyful noise!

•Use a prism (or unwanted CD) and a strong light source to make bright patterns on a wall.

Adults too

Tiddlywinks resources are published by Scripture Union and on the cover, you will find the logo of a lamp, which in various designs has been used since SU began in 1867. Chief executive Keith Civval says: 'The lamp has always stood for our belief that the Bible has the power to light our way and guide us in how to live, as it says in the Psalms' (Psalm 119:105).

Scripture Union produces a wide range of materials to help you to engage with the Bible: personal Bible reading, group studies, Lent courses, and the church-wide New SALT programme for all ages. Online you can read the verse of the day, do a daily Bible reading and sign up for the church@home internet magazine for leaders of small groups. Contact information is on pages 89 and 96.

Top tip

Try this activity during any session: children enjoy it more as they become familiar with the idea.

Say you know a way to spread the love of God to everyone in the group. Explain that you know God loves you and that makes you feel very happy. What do we do when we're happy? Smile! Pass a smile round the circle: turn to the child on one side of you, smile; that child then turns to their neighbour and smiles. When the smile gets back to you, repeat in the other direction. Do any of the children want to start the smile going around?

When you've all smiled for each other, pray, thanking God for his love for us and that we can share his love with others. All do an extra-special smile for God!

ACTIVITY PAGE:
The photocopiable activity page for this outline is on page 88

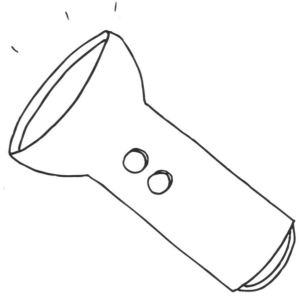

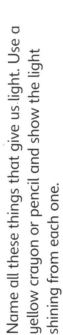

We need light to see by. Thank you, God, for making light.

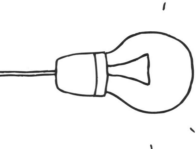

Name all these things that give us light. Use a yellow crayon or pencil and show the light shining from each one.

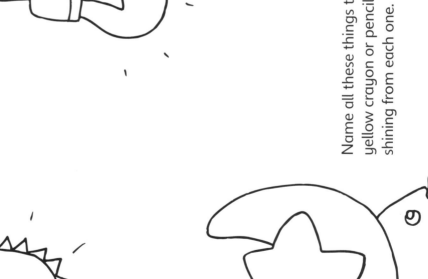

My name

First steps in Bible reading

The *Tiddlywinks* range of Little Books

My Little Red Book
First steps in Bible reading
Reese discovers Christmas is coming...
1 85999 659 0

My Little Yellow Book
First steps in Bible reading
Danny finds out about Easter.
1 85999 693 0

My Little Blue Book
First steps in Bible reading
Lucy and Liam find out All about me...
1 85999 660 4

My Little Green Book
First steps in Bible reading
Krista explores God's wonderful world
1 85999 696 5

My Little Purple Book
First steps in Bible reading
Lily discovers 'Jesus loves me'.
1 85999 720 1

Tiddlywinks Little Books are designed to be used at home by a parent/carer with an individual child. Linked to the themes covered in the *Tiddlywinks* Big Books, children can discover and learn about the Bible and share their discoveries with you. There are 50 first steps in Bible reading pages in each book, with a story for each day and extra activity pages of fun things to do. Children will love exploring the Bible with child characters Lucy and Liam, Reese, Danny, Krista and Lily.
A5, 64pp £3.50 each (Prices subject to change)

You can order these or any other *Tiddlywinks* resources from:
- Your local Christian bookstore
- Scripture Union Mail Order:
  Telephone 01908 856006
- Online: log on to
  www.scriptureunion.org.uk/tiddlywinks
  to order securely from our online bookshop

COMING SOON
My Little Orange Book

" When the Big Books are used in conjunction with the Little Books, children and adults encounter an attractive mixture of stories and activities that will encourage everybody to know and trust in Jesus. "
Diana Turner,
Editor of *Playleader Magazine*

The flexible resource for pre-school children and carers

Also now on sale!
Glitter and Glue. Pray and Play.
Even more craft and prayer ideas for use with under fives

Have a family fun day

Jonah 1–3

This event is designed for children under five years old with their parents or other supervising adults. Children under two and a half are still included, but will need more adult supervision.

The event is designed to last for up to 90 minutes: if you have less time available, omit some of the activities and shorten the time allowed for 'Creative fish activities'.

Registration

(20 minutes)

Begin approximately 10 minutes before the start time, depending on how many are expected. Appoint a registration team to be in the registration area for twenty minutes over the start time. They should keep an eye out for late arrivals during the session. It is always helpful to register age of children, address, contact number for follow up invitation events and fire/safety regulations.

Programme

Creative fish activities
(30 minutes)

Set up these areas around the hall or in smaller rooms, using tables surrounded by chairs. Ideally, they should be child-sized tables and chairs. Have each activity supervised by a team member while children and 'their' adults rotate around the activity areas. A sample of each activity can be helpful, but do encourage children to express their own ideas. Parents or carers can assist the children with creating and finish off activities if a child requests it. Creations should be named, if possible, for identification and collection later so they could be left on display until the end of the session.

Organise up to five activity areas:

Foam fish: cut different coloured foam sheets into squiggly pieces for weeds and different sized fish shapes, ready for the children to stick on to pale blue A4 card.

Play dough sea life: coloured play dough can be shaped into various sea creatures (starfish, boats) using moulds, cutters or hands.

Sticker fish: draw bold outlines of fish shapes on sheets of A3 or A4 paper. Give children self-adhesive coloured stickers and washable, chunky felt-tip pens to create their own fish designs.

Finger boats: draw simple boat shapes and waves onto A3 paper. Let children dab on finger paints to decorate. Make sure you have damp cloths available for cleaning hands.

Fish collage: draw large fish outlines, including eyes, fins and tail, on large pieces of card. Stick on scrunched-up coloured tissue or crêpe paper with glue.

Bubbles burst
(5 minutes)

Suggest that the children pretend to be swimming around under water. Have several adults strategically placed blowing bubbles into the room above their heads. Ask the children to pop as many of the bubbles as they can to some music. This will capture something like the bubble effect under water.

Find fish puzzle
(5 minutes)

Make a large floor jigsaw puzzle (several, in different colours, if you expect a lot of children) by cutting body, head, tail and fins from coloured card/paper. Hide the pieces beforehand or during the earlier creative activities. Encourage adults to assist children in finding the pieces and then assembling the puzzles.

Refreshments
(5 minutes)

Enjoy a drink and a biscuit together. Biscuits could be home-made in fish shapes. Have a short break to keep the programme moving.

• Keep children out of kitchen areas.

• Don't carry trays of hot drinks into areas where children are playing.

• Sit the children down to have their drinks.

• Use feeder beakers for younger ones and half-full plastic cups for those a little older.

• Have alternatives available for children who may have allergies or react to food or drink additives.

Puppets and visual story
(10 minutes)

Using an animal puppet (a fish made from a sock, with shiny fabric fins sewn on), ask the children to come and sit in a defined area. The puppet tells the Jonah story from the point where Jonah is

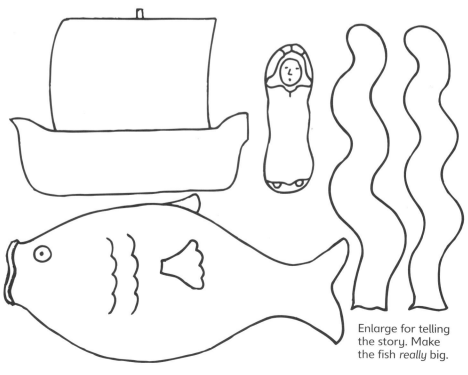

Enlarge for telling the story. Make the fish *really* big.

trying to walk away from God. It describes the scene in the story using these key objects: Jonah, boat, sea, fish, sand. As each is mentioned, place the appropriate visual on a large display board. (Use a small self-adhesive Velcro patch to hold it in position.) The puppet explains that, after three days inside the fish, Jonah was spat out on to the beach. The puppet laughs and encourages all the children to laugh. Jonah went and obeyed God. Ask the children if they like to obey their mum and dad?

If you are not confident telling the story in your own words, use a children's Bible or the Story time option from *Tiddlywinks: The Big Orange Book*.

Tunnel crawl
(5 minutes)

Have two play tunnels taped together so that the children can crawl through. Explain that it could be like crawling through the mouth of a big fish!

Parachute story
(10 minutes)

You will need: *play parachute or sheet; large beach ball; small, soft lightweight balls; foam bath toys.*

Mushroom the parachute and call a child's name to run under it. This can highlight that God loves each child and knows us by name.

Place a large inflated beach ball (with drawn boat on it) on the chute and see if the adults (kneeling) and children can

work together to enable the ball to move around the outside of the chute by tilting and lifting when appropriate. Then, try bouncing the ball as high as you can in the air. Hold the chute out fairly taut and let young children go underneath, one at a time, and try to knock the ball off the canopy.

Whilst doing this, one person can tell the story of a man named Jonah who tried to run away from God and jumped on a boat… Remove the large ball once Jonah has been thrown overboard and throw on lots of little balls. Bounce them as high as you can: these can be air bubbles from fish in the sea and one fish in particular.

To illustrate what it was like inside the fish, bring the chute over your heads, down your backs and sit on it. One adult stands in the middle as a tent pole. Children can wave to each other inside the chute. Mention how, in the Jonah story, Jonah was inside a large fish for three days. Some fish and other underwater plastic bath toys could be used as props inside! Of course, Jonah was spat out…

Stress that God was with Jonah and knew where he was all the time. God kept him safe inside the fish.

Music
(7 minutes)

Celebrate having a happy day with song, music and movement. Young children can learn the actions even if they are too young to pick up the words. Choose from:

'My God is so big', *KS* 255
'If you're happy and you know it clap your hands', (make up some additional verses, using ideas suggested by the children).
'Have you seen the pussy cat?' *KS* 100
'God's love is deeper', *KS* 84
'Wide, wide as the ocean', *JU* p72
'What noise shall we make?' *KS* 369

Jonah collage
(10 minutes)

Make plenty of boat, sea, fish, sand and seaweed shapes (as used for the story but smaller scale); give one of each to a child with a background sheet of blue or green card. Let them assemble a picture and fix it in place using glue. Give help if necessary but allow and encourage the children to do as much as they can themselves.

Party bags
(3 minutes)

Prepare home time gift bags with seaside-themed novelties (fish-shaped savoury biscuits, fondant prawns, chocolate shells) and a copy of *Jonah*, a Little Fish book from Scripture Union. (You might like to have a few bags with different books, so siblings do not have the same. Also have alternatives available for children who may have allergies or react to food additives.)

Top tips

•Check your venue is safe for under-fives. Pay particular attention to eye and head level sharp objects, cupboard corners, and trailing wires. Keep doors onto car parks or roads shut.

•Prepare well beforehand, collecting items in advance, buying resources, having the right amount of team members to run the event effectively.

•Design your programme to be varied, colourful and flexible.

•Advertise your event appropriately with suitable flyers given out a minimum of two weeks in advance.

•When using puppets, have someone to work off the puppets to the audience: this will give you greater control of response and behaviour. That person can also place the visuals in place on the board at the relevant points. If you do not have a puppet theatre, operate the puppets behind an overturned table, behind an armchair or between curtains. Alternatively, cradle the fish puppet in your arms and let it 'whisper' to you and then you convey what it said to the children. Have the children sit behind a certain line in a defined area and ask them not to go beyond the line.

•Use a tape recording as backing music to sing along to, if you do not have musicians who can accompany you.

•Use loop nylon as a covering for a simple display board. Use adhesive Velcro (hook and loop fastener) patches to fix visual aids to the board.

Welcome time

The beginning of a session is a busy time, with everyone arriving, meeting friends, setting out equipment, preparing refreshments and maybe taking money. Greeting the children and the adults who bring them is a time when you can really make them feel welcome and part of the group. The ideas given on these pages aim to give you a structure for this.

You could use a different welcome time idea each time you meet. Or select one which suits your group and use it to launch your time together every session. This will help build a sense of group identity so that even very young children will start to join in with a regular and repeated introduction. It could become the signal for the group to come together, and the children will learn that they should be quiet and still for the next activity.

Your group may not have a specific start time – so save your welcome time for when the whole group comes together, maybe for singing or a story, or before refreshments.

If you start at a set time, have an informal sing-song or news sharing for a few minutes before your regular welcome time, so that anyone arriving late does not miss out.

Tiddlywinks: The Big Purple Book has ideas for welcoming everyone to your group, plus extra ways of welcoming new children or visitors, saying a positive 'hello' to parents and carers, and for celebrating birthdays.

Turn to pages 94 and 95 for home time ideas.

There are more welcome time ideas in other 'Big Books' in the *Tiddlywinks* range.

Welcome time idea 1

I'm here!
Use individual registration cards for the children, each with a different picture to make it easy for the children to recognise their own. Have the cards spread out on a table near the entrance. When they arrive, the children find their card and post it in a box with a slit like a letter box. This both helps you with registration and involves the child right from the start of the session.

If attendance is less regular or where different children come on different days/weeks, have a bowl full of coloured clothes pegs. When the child arrives, they clip a peg next to their name or picture on a length of string attached to the wall to say, 'I'm here today'.

Welcome time idea 2

God made me and you
This is an active rhyme encouraging everyone to move about and to improvise movements. Speak firmly and clearly with a definite rhythm. Choose from the verses suggested, and make up and add your own which are special to your group. After each verse, allow a few moments for everyone to jump, clap, dance or whatever.

> God made me and you,
> I can jump, how about you?
>
> God made me and you,
> I can clap, how about you?
>
> God made me and you,
> I can dance, how about you?
>
> God made me and you,
> I can skip, how about you?
>
> God made me and you,
> I can pray, how about you?
>
> God made me and you,
> I can sing, how about you?
>
> God made me and you,
> I can love, how about you?

Happy Birthday

Start with the whole group together and then divide up into smaller groups, by age. When you have all the two-year-olds, three-year-olds, etc, sitting together, show how the birthday child is going to be moving from one 'age' to another. Say something like, 'Ian was three and now he's going to be four!' while Ian moves from the three-year-olds to the four-year-olds. Some children may appreciate an adult to hold their hand and lead them as they move; others will be there before you know it! Then all sing 'Happy birthday' and clap out the age of the child.

Welcome time idea

3

Who is here today?
You will need: a large piece of fabric.

Settle children in a circle, with their parent or carer. Choose a confident child or ask for a volunteer to start the welcome game. Use the fabric to drape over the child or for the child to stand behind. Younger children or those who are less sure can take an adult with them!

All sing to the tune of 'Frère Jacques', putting in the name of the child and your own group.

> Where is Kate? Where is Kate?
> Has she come? Has she come?
> Has she come to Tiddlywinks?
> Has she come to Tiddlywinks?

(Lift the fabric revealing the child.)

> Yes, she has. Yes, she has.

Repeat with other children. End with all the children under or behind the fabric while the adults sing: 'Where are all the children...?'

Welcome time idea

4

Hello
Each time you meet, choose a different way to all say 'hello' to each other. Demonstrate how to do this with a few children (or all of them, if the group is fairly small). Then let the children move around the room and when they meet one another, use today's greeting. Write the options on cards and make choosing a card the introduction to the game.

You could: shake hands; bow from the waist; smile and wave; give a friendly high one-hand clap; 'air kiss' both cheeks; or say 'hello' in different languages.

Here are some to get you started.

French	Bonjour	Bohn-ZHOOR
German	Guten Tag	Goo-ten-TAHG
Mandarin Chinese	Nihao	NEE how
Hawaiian	Aloha	a-LOH-ha
Hindi	Namaste	Na-MAH-stay
Hebrew	Shalom	Sha-LOME
Portuguese	Olá	Oh-LAH
Spanish	Buenos días	BWAY-nos DEE-ahs
Swahili (Kenya, Tanzania)	Jambo	JAHM-bo
Yoruban (Nigeria, Benin, Togo)	Bawoni	BAH-who-nee

Welcome to adults

A full but not messy notice board can give plenty of useful information and even be a conversation starter. Monitor your board and make sure any posters are up to date, news is current and you haven't got five notices using one drawing pin!

Include:

- Information about your group
- Local facilities (swimming pool, toddler events, party entertainers)
- Church events which will interest both children and adults
- For sale and wanted cards
- Press cuttings which might be of interest.

If you can't have a permanent board, make a lightweight portable one by gluing together several layers of thick cardboard and covering the surface with loose-weave fabric, so pin holes don't show.

Make sure any pinboard is out of reach of the children.

Welcome to new children or visitors

Work with the children who are regulars in the group to make a 'welcome book' for newcomers. Talk with them about the activities they enjoy and the things they like doing. Write down their comments, keeping to their own wording as much as possible. Type up these comments and print them out on individual pages, leaving plenty of space for children to add drawings. Let them illustrate the pages, using strong colours which can be photocopied. Copy and collate finished pages. If you have facilities nearby, children may be able to watch the photocopying. Involve the children as much as possible in collating the books by giving each child a pile of the same page to hold; line the children up in page order and then work your way along, taking one page from each child. Staple the books together or punch holes and tie with a length of ribbon or string.

Make several copies of your book, which can be given to new children or visitors to look through or keep.

Home time

The end of a session can be chaotic, with some people in a rush to leave, others still chatting, children tired and fractious or still full of energy and reluctant to be strapped into a buggy or to put their coat on. Leaders may be busy clearing up and cleaning up. But a positive home time can make each person feel they are valued, and encourage them to come next time.

You could use a different home time idea each time you meet. Or select one which suits your group and use that to close your time together every session. This will help build a sense of group identity so that even very young children will start to join in with a regular and repeated 'goodbye'.

If you finish at a set time, select a home time activity to use as the last item of your programme. Make sure you allow enough time so that people don't have to hurry off or miss this part. If your group is less structured, choose a time when you are all together, towards the end of the session. Make home time a definite event and avoid having people putting away equipment or clearing up at the same time: aim to include and involve everyone.

Tiddlywinks: The Big Purple Book has ideas for saying 'goodbye' to everyone in your group, ways of marking 'milestone' events: those going to a new area or leaving the group to start school; and a suggestion for calming a lively or disruptive group when you want to settle them for a quieter or listening activity.

Turn back to pages 92 and 93 for welcome time ideas.

There are more home time ideas in other 'Big books' in the *Tiddlywinks* range.

1

Home time idea

Say it or sing it
Learn and say this prayer together, putting the name of your own group into the last line.

> Dear God, thank you for each happy day,
> For fun, for friends and work and play.
> Thank you for your loving care,
> At Tiddlywinks, home and everywhere.

And sing as you go, to the tune of 'Frère Jacques':

> Thank you Jesus, thank you Jesus,
> We love you, we love you.
> Thank you for our playgroup,
> Thank you for our playgroup,
> A-amen, a-amen.

2

Home time idea

See you soon
Gather together in a circle at the end of the session. Hand out any craft or other items the children need to take home, making a positive comment each time. Sing this song (substituting the appropriate day and activities) to the tune of 'This old man, he played one' to remind everyone of what you have done together:

> Friday's here, Friday's here!
> Friday's here, now is that clear?
> Painting, sticking, haven't we had fun?
> Lots to do for everyone!

Follow with a song which rounds up the day and also looks forward to next time. The tune is 'Twinkle, twinkle little star'.

> Now it is the end of play,
> All the toys have gone away.
>
> Hope you had a lovely play,
> See you all another day.
> Now it is the end of play,
> See you all another day.

3

Home time idea

Wave bye-bye
Finish with this active song and game, to the tune of 'London Bridge'. Use the name of your own group. Add other verses if you wish, but always end with 'wave bye-bye'.

> Tiddlywinks are falling down, falling down, falling down,
> Tiddlywinks are falling down, all fall down!
>
> Tiddlywinks are bouncing up, bouncing up, bouncing up,
> Tiddlywinks are bouncing up, bounce up tall.
>
> Tiddlywinks wave bye-bye, wave bye-bye, wave bye-bye,
> Tiddlywinks wave bye-bye, see you next week.

<... >
</...>

Home time idea

Goodbye

Use the same method or language as the Welcome time 'Hello' idea on page 93.

Here are some ways to say 'goodbye' in different languages to get you started. Children love playing with words and they'll soon grasp unusual sounds – especially if they understand the meaning too.

French	Au revoir	Oh ruh-VWAH
German	Auf Wiedersehen	Owf VEED-er-zane
Mandarin Chinese	Zài jiàn	Dzay jenh
Hawaiian	Aloha	a-LOH-ha
Hindi	Namaste	Na-MAH-stay
Hebrew	Shalom	Sha-LOME
Portuguese	Adeus	Ah-deh-OOSH
Spanish	Adiós	Ah-dee-OSE
Swahili (Kenya, Tanzania)	Kwaheri	Kwa-HAYR-ee
Yoruban (Nigeria, Benin, Togo)	Odabo	Oh-DAH-bo

4

Quiet and calm...

When you want to settle the children together for circle time or a story, don't get caught in the trap of yelling 'Be quiet!' above a hubbub of noise! Remove other distractions: make 'tidy-up time' a joint task which will signify that one phase of the session is over and another beginning. Invite the children to join you on a carpet or sitting together; then wait. Have at least one helper to round up the children.

Once most children are together, use some quietening actions to calm their bodies and their voices. You could ask them all to pretend to be tiny seeds (curled down on the floor) and talk them through growing and moving gently in the breeze. Or suggest they lie on the floor with their eyes shut while you mention things for them to listen out for: can you hear that car outside? Or the baby crying in the next room? Then say: 'In a few moments I'm going to ask you to open your eyes... open your eyes... in a few moments I'm going to say you can sit up slowly... slowly... sit up slowly...hello everybody.' Keep your voice quiet and calm so the children have to concentrate on listening to you, rather than making a noise themselves. It won't work first time – but keep trying!

Moving away

So long, farewell
Construct a leaving ceremony using one or any combination of these ideas.

● Make the child and/or family a card and present it.

● Sing 'Happy leaving to you' to the tune of 'Happy birthday'.

● Present them with a certificate to mark their time with you, or a folder of their work and photos and messages from the group.

● Have a special treat such as cake instead of biscuits at refreshment time.

● Give the child a memento: a bookmark, balloon or small book.

● Pray for the children individually: 'Thank you God for Jack. Please bless him in his new home. Amen.'

Get Ready Go

A child's first day at school is a big moment for them... and you. But while some children can't wait to get started, others might not be so confident. Making sure your children are ready to go is really important.

Get Ready Go! is a brilliant new book for children about to start primary school. Using simple words, bright pictures and fun activities, Get Ready Go! explains what school is going to be like, helping your children prepare for that exciting first term.

Get Ready Go! comes complete with a companion guide for parents, packed with useful advice so that you can help them get ready too.

Get Ready Go! is a great new resource for all Early Years educators and can also be used by primary schools as a central part of their induction programme.

A colourful three-book set in an envelope, available singly or in packs of 10. Each set contains:

Get Ready to Let Go

'Have I put enough in her lunchbox?' Essential preparation for families and parents.

Get Ready Go!

'What's it going to be like?' A clear, friendly guide to help children talk and think about the big adventure of starting school!

God Knows

A 'Little Fish' picture book to reassure children that God knows them and is with them at all times – even on their first school day!

Individual set – £4.99 ISBN 1 85999 592 6
Pack of 10 – £25.00 ISBN 1 85999 588 8

Have you enjoyed this book?

Then take a look at the other Big Books in the *Tiddlywinks* range. Why not try them all?

The Big Purple Book
Themes: Jesus loves me; God loves it when I... make music, sing, dance, look at books, I'm 'me'; Friends and followers; Materials and technology
1 85999 719 8

The Big Red Book
Themes: Christmas is coming; People we meet; Stories Jesus told; God gives us food
1 85999 658 2

The Big Blue Book
Themes: All about me; God gives us... homes, clothes, food, etc; People who knew Jesus; Friends of God
1 85999 657 4

'I love this! It's great!' Sarah, leader of a 3 to 5s group in Victoria, Australia.

Tiddlywinks Big Books are designed for use in any pre-school setting. The multi-purpose outlines are packed full of play, prayers, crafts, stories and rhymes; simply pick and mix ideas to meet the particular needs of your group. You'll find plenty of practical advice on setting up and running a pre-school group, plus ideas in every session to help you include adult carers. The children will love the illustrated activity pages.

A4, 96pp, £8.99 each (Prices subject to change)

You can order these or any other *Tiddlywinks* resources from:

- Your local Christian bookstore
- Scripture Union Mail Order: Telephone 01908 856006
- Online: log on to **www.scriptureunion.org.uk/tiddlywinks** to order securely from our online bookshop

The Big Yellow Book
Themes: Easter; God gives us families; Friends of Jesus; What's the weather like?
1 85999 692 2

The Big Green Book
Themes: God's wonderful world; God gives us people; Let's find out about Jesus; God knows when I'm... happy, cross, sad, scared, busy
1 85999 695 7

'...really pleased with your material and look forward to integrating Tiddlywinks into our existing programme.' Marion, Scotland

Also now on sale!
Glitter and Glue. Pray and Play.
Even more craft and prayer ideas for use with under fives